Run The Race of Life – The Real Way

The "Lenny Livright" Story

Run The Race of Life
The Real Way

Discover the Power and Purpose of Christian Living
The "Lenny Livright" Story

Jim Biscardi, Jr.

Contents

Forward

Jesus promised that He would return – and for centuries Christians have been looking heavenward wondering, "Could this be the day?" As Christians, we reach the point of no return, when we realize that we are in the midst of a race that will only terminate when we are in the presence of our Lord. In this race, there will be many evil forces that will endeavor to knock us out of the race by stumbling us, deceiving us, and even knocking us down.

Jim Biscardi, Jr. tells of Satan's attack in the church to lure believers away from the foundation of the Word of God – to knock them out of the race that is before them. I am pleased with this book, *Run The Race of Life – The Real Way,* because it teaches the believer that with trust in God, and in His Word, we will finish the race victoriously.

It also excites me to know that I do not have to *win* the race, I only have to finish it. When I do, I become more than a conqueror.

Reverend John DelTurco
General Overseer
The Christian Church of North America

"Therefore, since we are surrounded by such a great cloud of witnesses, let us throw off everything that hinders and the sin that so easily entangles, and let us run with perseverance the race marked out for us. Let us fix our eyes on Jesus, the Pioneer and Perfecter of our faith…"

Hebrews 12: 1-2

Introduction

Christians and non-Christians alike are wondering what life is really meant to be. People are dismayed and frustrated as they run the race of life. Knowledge has expanded faster in the last fifty years than in all of man's existence. Yet, with all of our scientific and technological accomplishments, as well as our financial prosperity, we have senseless murders, rapes, kidnapping, thefts, and other extraordinary cruel crime – even children are murdering other children. Schools have been forced to close down after mass killings by students. The broken survivors of this hate and anger need psychological help to recover. Teen pregnancy and abandoning or murdering infants shock us. Killing the unborn has become commonplace. Our prosperity can't help us. Throwing money into advertising campaigns, hiring more people, and creating new programs to correct these and the ever-present compulsive disorders (e.g. the alcohol and drug problems) have not resulted in significant improvements.

Our television and radio programs, movies, and music, which usually reflect the attitudes of our day are mainly about the horror of people rising from the dead, killing, investigating the worlds beyond in outer space, illicit sex, and pocket monsters. These reflect how far we have gone "off track" – outside the boundaries set by our loving heavenly Father to find life, liberty, and the pursuit of happiness. But that's what's happening in our world. These also suggest that people are searching more intensely than ever before for something beyond themselves. A popular television program, *Touched By An Angel*, which portrays God's loving intervention in people's lives, was slated to be terminated by network executives until audiences petitioned the station. At the other extreme, psychic phenomenon and programs with psychics as regular guests, receiving listener calls for advice, have become very popular as well. In pursuit of the illusive "gold medal" to satisfy our inner spiritual quest, numerous cults and false religions have covered the world's "racetrack". These are really "pot holes", faults in the earth, and crumpling footholds – traps that are cleverly disguised with truth but end in defeat and death. Like rats that go for the food that covers the trap below, cult members are beckoned onward by false hopes and promises. Many cults quote the Bible and preach a partial gospel. They talk about prayer, Jesus, and the Bible. But underneath this layer of truth is the trap of error. Jehovah's Witness, the Mormons, Scientology, and the Unification Church are a few examples. David Koresh, gathered about 130 followers at "Ranch Armageddon" in Waco Texas. Calling himself a "sinful" incarnation of Jesus, he talked of government conspiracies and told followers that women were exclusively for his sexual gratification and procreation. In 1993, a 51-day siege between the Davidians and federal authorities ended in killing Koresh and 81 followers. Jim Jones led hundreds to their death in Guyana South America. The Order of the Solar Temple, led by Luc Jouret, was unknown until 1994 when more than 50 members, including Jouret, killed themselves in Canada and Switzerland. Jouret had persuaded them to give up their jobs and turn assets over to the cult. More suicides followed in 1995 and 1996. Marshall Applegate and 38 followers of the Heaven's Gate cult committed suicide in 1997. Applegate won converts in the 70's with a doctrine woven from science fiction, millennialism, and Christianity. The group believed that a UFO following comet Hale-Bopp would take them to a higher level of existence. Man is following man instead of following Christ. Man's "progress" hasn't given men and women a solid track to run upon or a course to guide them through the tragedy, darkness, uncertainty, and frustration.

This seems to be the age of deception. Christians, not rooted and grounded in Bible truth, are being deceived. Christians, unaware of how to keep their Christian lives connected to Christ, seem bewildered and unable to cope with things that happen to them and their loved ones. There's persecution for what seems like no reason at all; families being torn apart; splits in churches and between individual Christians because of unforgiveness; there's politics for "spiritual profit"; immorality of church leaders; denominational boundaries and distrust of others; and a drift by many away from organized Christianity. Christians want and must have answers. "What's this Christian life really all about? Are there boundaries and course markers to help us stay on track? What's the goal and where's the finish line? What should we expect when we stand or run for Christ?

Yet Christian believers do have the Answer. We have the great Starter, Forerunner, Finisher and Victor of life's most important race.

We should be leading others through these dark days – influencing people all around us and making disciples for Christ. The times we are experiencing may be judgments of God - the fertile soil needed for a last ingathering of souls – God's huge fishing net. Christians need to be different – peculiar people – in their relationship with God. Instead of worshipping the idols of technology, science, prosperity, education, and material possessions, we need to be transformed by the renewing of our minds. We need to more intimately know and emulate Christ – to embrace His values and behaviors that are found in the cross of Christ. We must be strong and courageous in running this marathon. And encourage others to follow us as we follow Christ – as we run for Christ in His strength, not our own. To be effective in making disciples, however, believers need to understand and better articulate some basic concepts and truths about the Christian life.

Here are some of them:

- How to simply describe the essence of man
- What it means to be born-again. What's the "old man"? What's the "natural man" or "the flesh"?
- How to correctly describe the "kingdom of God" and the entrance requirements.
- How to clearly explain the "what" and "why" of a believer's total human experience – including the trials and tribulations
- How to keep our eyes upon Christ and grow spiritually (i.e. how to keep the Christian life connected to Christ).
- How to describe our Lord Jesus Christ and the Christian life to unbelievers without the rhetoric and the "Christian vocabulary".
- How to make disciples by emulating Christ? What's the process of being "transformed" into His image? Is there a prescribed diet of the right nourishment and an exercise plan of proper discipline?
- How to work "for" Him and simultaneously work "from" Him?
- Is heaven our final destination? If not, then where? What's the prize and goal of this Christian race? How is the race here preparing us for what we will do in eternity?
- What should be a Christian's view of eternity?

Run The Race of Life – The Real Way is about the Christian race. It explains these and other important truths. Besides depending heavily upon Biblical references, the story of Lenny Livright personalizes the strain, struggles, and joy to run God's way. The strength of this work is in its simple circles that describe complex truths. They help us all to understand, live, and explain the Christian life more effectively – especially to unbelievers. Because of these illustrations, this work could have been called, "Getting Around In Christian Circles". My hope is that the words and illustrations will be used for one-on-one witnessing, small group Bible studies, and also more formal programs of Christian education – all for fulfilling the Great Commission in making disciples for Christ.

Pressing Toward The Finish Line With You - In Christ,
Jim Biscardi, Jr.

Chapter 1

Roar Of The Crowd
The Old Paradigm

This is the story Lenny Livright. He lived in a nice neighborhood in a big city. It wasn't in any way considered a rich area because most of the people who settled there were immigrants from Europe – mostly Italians and Irish. Lenny Livright was the big brother to his sister Louise. He thought the neighborhood was the best – a playground around the corner, wide streets, woods behind the house next door, and plenty of cousins living in the same house. His dad and mom wanted him to have all the advantages of a young man that they weren't able to have growing up.

His parents sent him to church and made sure that he attended all the religious prerequisites for being accepted in that community. At Christmas, you'd never know that the Livrights were poor because Lenny's mom would save every penny to make that morning the most marvelous moment in the year. There was nothing and no one that meant more to Lenny than his mom and dad. Discipline was never a problem – just a word from his mom and a look from his dad were sufficient.

Whether it was baseball, biking, or books, Lenny understood that he needed to be the best. Practice, study, achievement awards, recognition, being first in everything was the way to success. His mom lovingly assured him after every game and whenever he would bring his report card home from school that he WAS the best. Getting a "B" or "C" might be good enough for others, but Lenny had to get the "A" – nothing else would please his parents. And Lenny didn't let them down – He was valedictorian at his

Junior High School graduation and among the top ten and president of the National Honor Society at his high school graduation.

Lenny's dad sold his life insurance policy to raise enough money to send him to college. He never had many friends because he had this incessant drive to achieve. Lenny knew that he might be drawn into the Vietnam conflict – and it would be easier he reasoned as an officer – so he joined Air Force ROTC. He studied long hours and had very little time for socializing, fraternities, dances, and parties. He was, however, faithful in attending church every Sunday. His grades in college earned him a scholarship from the Air Force to attend New York University for his Masters degree. He married the first girl who gave him any real attention. And a few years later found himself in Vietnam with a wife and two children back home.

He was scared and very lonely in Vietnam. He found the way to success was to be a little bit better than everyone else – a lot of drinking, cursing, gambling, and "big talk" – in between giving the fighter pilots the latest intelligence and debriefing them after their bombing missions. He even won the Bronze Star for meritorious service because he invented a way to communicate information back to headquarters faster than anyone else.

Lenny Livright never stopped being faithful to attend chapel. One day, while playing darts with another Air Force Captain, Lenny began to complain vigorously about a fellow airman. To the point where his companion reminded Lenny of what he had heard many times in his religious training, "Don't you know you're supposed to love your neighbor?" Well at that point Lenny let it all hang out and he told his companion, "Love my neighbor? Who's my neighbor? You mean those drunks who lie, cheat, and steal everything that's not locked down…those drug-dealing, murderers who could care less for me and my life? That's who my neighbor is. And I can't ever love them!"

The Roar of the Crowd – *Biblical Principals and Application*

Before the race begins, every athlete does some stretching exercises. These limbering up exercises put our muscles into shape so we can bring them under control and use them to the fullest to win the race. In life, there are many influences to which we are exposed. Each one is "stretching" us

Behaviors
Values
World View

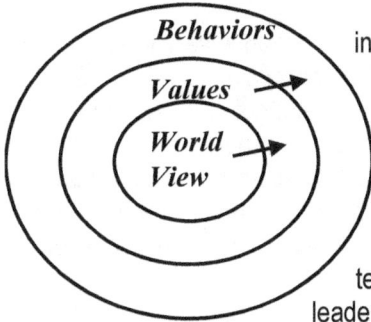

into various shapes. I understand that even in the womb we are influenced by the music around us and by the temperament of our mothers. After we are born, we continue to be exposed to the roar of those who have major influences on our life – parents, teachers, friends, employers, church leaders. The television programs, the music we choose, the movies and pictures we expose ourselves to – all of these roar with what comes to be our standards for living and being successful. They shape our mentality or what's called our "world view" – the person (s) or things that our world spins around and who or what should receive our fullest attention and time. This view of our world then shapes what we deem important (i.e. our values) and these then determine our behaviors.

The Scriptures teach us that we are in a spiritual battle for our soul (i.e. our intellect, emotions, and will). There are "enemies" who want to exercise their influence on our lives. Who are these enemies? EPH 6:12 tells us that we do not fight against flesh and blood (i.e. other people) but against principalities and powers, against the rulers of the darkness of this world, against spiritual wickedness in high places." We are further instructed that we have three major sources who "roar" for influence in our lives – the world (JA 4:14), the flesh (JA4: 3), and the devil (JA4: 7).

The Flesh - It seems that by nature we all have a desire to control our world. From the beginning of our life, we turn to our own independent way, trying to control situations, the future, and people. We even try to control God. Since we can't, we end up frustrated, rebellious, and critical. This incessant need to be in control is rooted in excessive self-love. We are wildly in love with ourselves!

The Apostle Paul called this self-centeredness "the flesh" (RO 8:12). It can also be called "the natural man". By nature, we live as though we owe the flesh our obedience. Paul also told Timothy what man was like, "For men shall be lovers of their own selves, covetous, boasters, proud, blasphemers, disobedient to parents, unthankful, unholy...lovers of pleasures more than lovers of God." (2TI 3:2-5)

The Devil - "Be sober, be vigilant; because your adversary the devil, as a roaring lion, walketh about seeking whom he may devour.."(1PE 5: 8). This enemy specializes in deceiving us. He is the father of liars. He will keep us convinced that we are good just the way we are. There's no need to seek God. There's no need to consider anyone but ourselves. This world is our "oyster". "Eat, drink and be merry for tomorrow we die." The devil "roars" with things of the world and the flesh to keep "self" in the center of our thinking.

The World - Regarding the "roar" of the world, 1JN 2: 16 says, "The lust of the eyes, the lust of the flesh, and the pride of life are not of the Father but of the world." These all can be seen during a time in the ministry of Jesus when He was tempted by the devil in the desert (LK 4:1-13).

- **The lust of the eyes** – LK 4: 5-8. The devil took Jesus up to a high mountain. From there, he showed Him all the kingdoms of this world in a brief moment of time. The devil then told Jesus that he would give Him all the power and glory of them if Jesus would only worship him.

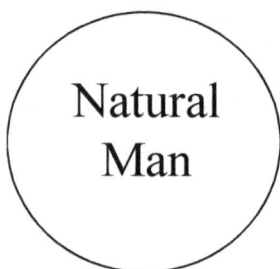

Jesus refused and told the devil, "Thou shalt worship the Lord thy God, and Him only shalt thou serve." Many people "see" power, influence, recognition, and position for themselves as things worthy enough to surrender their lives for.

Natural Man

Adam Before The Fall

- **The lust of the flesh** – LK 4: 3-4. Jesus was physically hungry after fasting for forty days. The devil challenged Him to prove He was the Son of God by changing the stones into bread. Jesus answered, "Man shall not live by bread alone, but by every word of God." For many of us, it's the material things that get our life – the delicacies of life fill our appetites and desires – food, houses, cars, sex, money, education, travel, etc. Our appetites will determine what we become over time.

- **The pride of life** – LK 4: 9-12. The devil brought Jesus to the pinnacle of the temple in Jerusalem and he challenged Him to throw Himself off and let the angels catch Him so that he could boast of His greatness in being the Son of God. But Jesus reminded this deceiver that, "Thou shalt not tempt the Lord thy God." Some of us are influenced to pursue greatness in some area to be able to boast or have others flood us with compliments and honors to boost our ego.

Natural
Man

Old Man Under The
Control Of Sin

Adam After The Fall

It may help us understand better about the "roar of the crowd" if we consider what man was like when he was first created. He was a natural man – with body, soul, and spirit. This natural man, or the flesh as we called it above, could act independently and make decisions. He had a free will, wisdom, skill, intellect, eloquence, feelings, etc. When Adam and Eve sinned, however, this natural man was subjected to what scripture calls the "old man". The part of us that loved to sin – enjoyed it. In fact, this natural man was not only influenced by sin, but also came into the bondage of sin. The natural man actually served sin. RO 6: 6 explains what happens to this "old man" as a result of accepting the work of Christ which we'll cover in the next chapter. It says, "...that our old man is crucified with him, that the body of sin might be destroyed, that henceforth we should not serve sin."

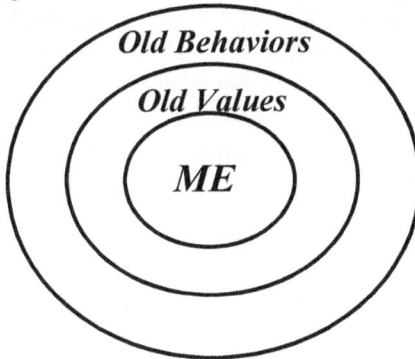

Old Behaviors
Old Values
ME

The "roar of the crowd" and the destruction done by the "old man" in our lives is like what locusts do to trees. When they attack a tree, they leave nothing of value on the tree. It's like a "hit and run" accident. They come in, and in 15 minutes eat up everything of value – even the bark. You go to sleep at night as a satisfied owner of a grove of productive trees. When you wake in the morning, your whole life is changed. You've lost everything – a victim of an unscrupulous predator that "hits and runs". Sin is like that. When sin comes in and is given full sway in a person's life, it leads to spiritual destruction of that life.

Think of how drugs ruin people's lives. The same is true about sins of the mind (e.g. impure or unwise thoughts and big egos), and of the heart (e.g. wrong attractions, appetites, desires, and illicit sex). Sins of envy, greed, and other sorts also destroy lives.

It's like the old time clothes wringer that squeezed every drop of water out of the wet clothes. Sin saps every drop of sincerity, real caring, real truth and fulfillment out of a life – often without the person realizing it. Life is empty and ruined. Reality becomes believing ones own lies and calling good evil and evil good. The worst tragedy is that it separates us from the greatest lover ever known – our heavenly Father, who created us to enjoy fellowship with Him.

Unless you are unlike most of us and able to resist the temptations cited above and "tune out" the roar of the crowd, then you – like us - were contaminated too and your world view had "self" in the center. Before coming to Christ, we are "stretched" to see ourselves at the center of everything.

This self-centered world view then shapes what we consider to be important in life – our values. If self is in the center of our world view, then what makes self look good or be successful is what we value. Further, whatever we value is what then determines how we behave. This combination of world view, values, and behaviors becomes our paradigm for living - all the rules for life and how we measure success. Here are a few of the old values many of us learn to consider very important and which form our paradigm for living before becoming Christians:

* Be Independent. Don't Depend on Others.

* Take Care of Yourself - Nobody Else Will

* Lead - Don't Follow

* Let Others Serve You - Don't You Serve Anyone

* Get to Know Only People Who Can Get You Ahead

* Don't Tell People Too Much About Yourself

* Use People - Love Things

* To Be Respected As a Leader, Throw You Weight Around

* The End Justifies the Means - Motives Don't Count

* Getting Is Better Than Giving

The crowd tells us that being independent and not dependent upon others is the goal for life. So we strive to become as wealthy as we can in material possessions. Get all that you can – can all that you get – and sit on the can! We also strive to build up our "network" of associations, who can get us what we want when we want it. And this "network" is usually made up of those who (like us) want to get ahead and consider us a stepping stone for doing that. We learn from the roar of the crowd how to use people and love material things. We begin to say that "It's who you know – not what you know - that leads to success and independence."

We also hear the crowd saying that serving self is essential. After all, if you don't help yourself then who will help you? We learn to get every advantage possible on our fellow human beings. Give yourself the best car, home, position, and education. And, if you couldn't go to the best school yourself, then at least send your kids. Give them the advantages for life that you didn't have. Helping others may some day be possible, but I come first and then those who are mine.

In addition, we make sure others know how great we are and how weak our competition is. We always act like the leader, the stronger, the highest, and the best. Maybe, if we act that way, people will believe it and want us as friends. And then we can use that friendship to get ahead. We learn to hide our weaknesses – our vulnerabilities – because there's always someone out there who will expose our weaknesses for their own gain. What's the difference if we lie, cheat, or steal a little to get ahead. If we don't do it, others will get ahead of us – maybe get the job that should be ours.

And if we ever get into a leadership position, be sure to make everyone know who's in charge. Use the "my way or the highway" mentality – throw your weight around. Use the "carrot and stick" philosophy of management – if they do what you want, reward them – if they disagree with you embarrass and abuse them. We tell ourselves, "These people now belong to us and they are here to follow orders and to make us look great as leaders so we can get ahead."

Chapter 2

Getting on Track
Born-Again New Creations

When Lenny's tour in Vietnam was up, he had saved enough money for a down payment on a new house near the Pentagon, where he was assigned. A brand smacking new house at 26 years old – things were really looking good for this medal winning, well educated, good father and husband. Nothing had changed, however, in terms of his opinion about neighbors – everybody was out to get him and take all of his accumulated possessions.

When Lenny was searching for his house, the realtor introduced him to one of the familes in the neighborhood – the Rightraks. They greeted him with warm smiles and a very special (almost joyful) feeling about him being there. Lenny liked the Mercedes-Benz he saw in the driveway, however with the exception of the man of the house, this family had strange first names: Esther & Joe had three kids – Eli, Rhonda, and Rachael. They also had a lot of Biblical sayings and pictures all over their house.

Lenny and his wife set about making friends with most of the "normal" neighbors. Every Friday night they went to the neighborhood party where there was plenty of drinking, loud music, and dancing. After a while, some of it was even too much for Lenny, but his wife liked it just fine and even stayed there while Lenny would put the kids to sleep. There were also big crab-catching parties on Saturdays where everyone dove into bushels of crabs and a keg of beer. But those Rightraks never showed up – very unfriendly people.

After about two years of that, Lenny's wife was diagnosed with a serious lower back problem that required an operation to fuse two disks together. A fluid was draining out and touching the nerves in her back and causing terrible and crippling pain. The doctor explained that the operation would take about 6 hours and there was a chance of permanent damage and paralysis. Lenny's world came tumbling down on him. His education, good job, nice family, medals, house, money and his other material possessions were of no help now.

But he still had his friends – they would help him get through all this. Suddenly, however, it seemed that the Livrights had caught a contagious disease – all his friends disappeared behind closed doors. Then something very strange happened. The Rightraks started to assure Lenny that everything would turn out fine because they were praying for his wife. They stayed in touch with Lenny and his family throughout the operation and recovery. They cooked meals for Lenny and the kids and they visited his wife in the hospital. They read the Bible to her and she told Lenny that it made her feel better. The operation was a success but something constantly plagued Lenny's mind – those Rightraks had showed so much love to a neighbor that hadn't done anything good for them. And their love was so sincere – even the kids helped! Then he remembered back two years before when his Vietnam buddy had challenged him to "love his neighbor". His neighbors were now really doing that to him – loving him.

One day when Lenny was alone with Esther, he asked her how she could love him and his family so much – especially since they had made fun of them because they never came to any of the parties. Esther said, "If you see any love in me, it's Jesus in me loving you." That's all she said. Well that's all Lenny had to hear. "Jesus in me", he thought. He concluded that if anyone should have Jesus in them it was him. He was a good man, lived right, and went to church. He couldn't get that thought out of his head. Finally, he searched through the Bible to get an explanation and seemed to find it in the Gospel of John chapter 10. He read where Jesus said, "I am the good shepherd: the good shepherd gives his life for the sheep...I am the good shepherd and know my sheep, and am known of mine."

He had never heard of such an intimate relationship between the Lord and people – or even understood what Christ's crucifixion meant for his life. But how could he get that relationship? He came across another verse in chapter 1 about "all those who received him, he gave them power to be children of God".

As Lenny was searching to understand all this, he had dream. In the dream, Lenny turned the corner in his home and Jesus stood before him. The Lord simply said, "Hi, Liv." When Lenny looked at His face, he was so frightened that he physically shook and woke up.

Then one day, mysteriously, Lenny found a book called **Prison to Praise** about a chaplain in Vietnam who led people to receive Jesus. It explained how to receive Christ. When he finished the book, without anyone else in the house, Lenny went into the bedroom and spoke these words to the Lord, "Lord, I'm not sure if I'm doing this right, but I really want you to be my savior and good shepherd. I realize now that I need you. I am sorry for my sins and I want to love others with your love. Please come into me so I can love others that way." He felt a big burden come off him in that moment. A sense of peace filled him and he knew that Jesus had taken residence in him.

Getting On Track – Biblical Principles and Application

The roar of the crowd not only creates the standards for living and being successful, but it also causes us to delude ourselves into thinking that we are something that we are really not. We walk around in this cloud of darkness. What we see is sadly not what's really there – we are figuratively blind to what is real – to what is true. We lie to ourselves and/or call our sins something that makes them sound "right for the new millennium." Selfish and evil people call themselves generous and good. Those in bondage to sin call themselves liberated. Those enjoying the folly of fools call themselves enlightened, and the lustful describe their sinful acts as love affairs.

It's as if we see the world upside down. Universities have actually researched the result of people seeing the world this way. They gave volunteers a pair of glasses to wear that turned everything upside down. At first, it was extremely difficult to adjust – so even the simplest things like walking and riding a bicycle were complicated and tiring. Then, as the volunteers spent time seeing things in this new way, even the normally difficult tasks became doable for them. It was unnerving, however, to learn that after they adjusted to viewing the world upside down the volunteers had a difficult job re-adjusting back to the normal way of seeing the world the way it really was! And that's the way it is with us. We have viewed the world so long based upon the roar of the crowd and our old paradigm, that re-adjusting to see the truth is difficult.

Not only do we believe that we are the most important person in the world – and that we must take care of me first – but we also believe that the world is there for our benefit – to serve us. Our life becomes a journey of seeing how much we can take from what's there – to possess whatever the roar of the crowd has convinced us is most important to have.

If we were to remain in that state of mind, the end of our journey would land us in Hell – and, while there, we'd probably complain about how unfairly such a victorious champion like ourselves was being treated. IS 5:20 warns us, "Woe to those who call evil good and good evil." Thank God, that He is Light and there is no darkness in Him. His Word is a lamp unto our feet and a light unto our path. Thank God, that He desires that no one should perish and that everyone should come to know the Truth.

He doesn't want anyone to remain wandering in that cloud of darkness. He has provided a way for every man, woman, and child to come out of the darkness and get onto the real race track of life. Jesus said, "I am come that they might have life, and that they might have it more abundantly." (JN 10:10). Thank God for creating an inner voice in each of us called a conscience. And thank Him for crises in life that make us wonder whether we are really as successful as we think.

Getting on this real race track involves the acceptance by faith of the following truths:

- "There is none righteous, no, not one." (RO 3:10). "All we like sheep have gone astray; we have turned every one to his own way..." (IS 53:6). All our righteousness (i.e. "right living") is as filthy rags to God, who is pure holiness. (IS 64:6)
- "For all have sinned and come short of the glory of God." (RO 3:23)
- "Your iniquities (i.e. sins) have separated between you and your God, and your sins have hid his face from you..."(IS 59:2)
- "Wherefore, as by one man (i.e. Adam) sin entered into the world, and death by sin; and so death passed upon all men, for that all have sinned." (RO 5:12)

But, there is a solution...

* "But God commends his love toward us, in that, while we were yet sinners Christ died for us." (RO 5:8)
* "For there is one God, and one mediator between God and men, the man Christ Jesus; who gave himself a ransom for all..." (1TI 2:5-6)
* "For the wages of sin is death; but the gift of God is eternal life through Jesus Christ our Lord." (RO 6:23)
* "Ye were... redeemed with the precious blood of Christ, as of a lamb without blemish and without spot." (1PE 1:18-19)
* "For whosoever shall call upon the name of the Lord shall be saved." (RO 10:13)
* "If thou shalt confess with thy mouth the Lord Jesus and shalt believe in thine heart that God hath raised him from the dead, thou shalt be saved." (RO10:9)
* "For with the heart man believeth unto righteousness; and with the mouth confession is made unto salvation... Whosoever believeth on him shall not be ashamed." (RO 10: 10-11)

When we accept these truths and sincerely ask Jesus to be our Savior and Lord, we are "receiving Jesus" and are "born-again"- literally "born from above". JN 1: 10-13 says that Jesus came unto his own and his own received him not. But to all those who received him, he gave them the power to become children of God – even those who believe in His name – who were born not of blood, nor the will of man, but born of God (i.e. born from above or born-again). We enter the family of God and (just like blood is common in earthly family members) God sends His Holy Spirit to take up residence in all believers (i.e. members of God's spiritual family).

We are "Christians" <u>only</u> when we have received Christ and are born-again.

There was a man of the Pharisee sect that came to Jesus at night named Nicodemas. He was a ruler of the Jews. He told Jesus that they knew He was a teacher sent from God. No one could do the miracles Jesus had done, Nicodemus said, unless God was with Him. This man was receiving/accepting Jesus only as a teacher but not for who He really was.

So Jesus said unto him, "Verily, verily, I say unto thee, Except a man be born again, he cannot see the kingdom of God." (JN 3:3)

Man is created in God's image. He is a triune being.

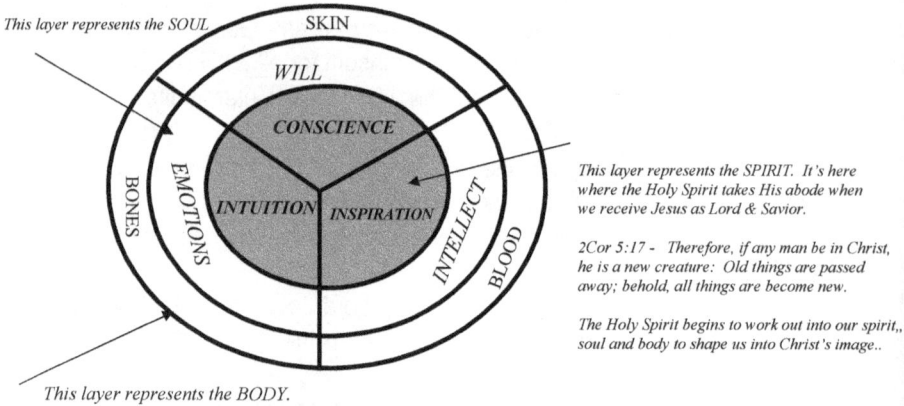

This layer represents the SOUL

SKIN

WILL

CONSCIENCE

BONES

EMOTIONS

INTUITION   *INSPIRATION*

INTELLECT

BLOOD

This layer represents the SPIRIT. It's here where the Holy Spirit takes His abode when we receive Jesus as Lord & Savior.

2Cor 5:17 - Therefore, if any man be in Christ, he is a new creature: Old things are passed away; behold, all things are become new.

The Holy Spirit begins to work out into our spirit,, soul and body to shape us into Christ's image..

This layer represents the BODY.

When we are "born-again", we are "saved" from the spiritual death sentence that God has imposed on those who sin, which includes everyone: "For the wages of sin is death; but the gift of God is eternal life through Jesus Christ our Lord". (RO 6:23).   Both the Old and New Testaments teach that there is life after death.   The patriarchs, the psalmists, the prophets, all pointed to the future. In Hebrews we read that Abraham looked for "a city…whose builder and maker is God." (HE 11:10) In 2COR 5:1, Paul wrote of "a building of God, an house not made with hands, eternal in the heavens." In GEN 5:24, Enoch "walked with God: and he was not for God took him." The Bible tells us that Elijah was taken up to heaven in a chariot of fire. (2 KI 2:11) The most powerful reason, however, for believing about life after death is the resurrection of Christ. It was witnessed by hundreds (1COR 15:3-7). Though we sense in ourselves that life must be more than just our existence here, Jesus proved once for all that there is life after death.

The resurrection gives meaning to the cross. The death of Christ is terrible news if it ends there. But because of His resurrection, it is "good news" – called "the Gospel". It assures us that His work is finished – that Christ atoned for everyone's sins. It also assures us that His work was perfect and that God was satisfied with His sacrifice – that Jesus was the "propitiation" for our sins. God demonstrated His satisfaction and confirmed Christ's work on the cross to atone for sin by raising Him from the dead (Acts 13:32-33).

Jesus said, "I am the resurrection, and the life: he that believeth in me though he were dead, yet shall he live: And whosoever that liveth and believeth in me shall never die." (JN 11:25-26). Salvation for you and me only requires our *repentance* of what *we* have done and our *acceptance* of what *Christ* has done for us. We "call upon the name of the Lord." God hears the cry of our repentant heart for forgiveness and "remembers" the work of His Son on our behalf. Our name is then written in heaven in the Lamb's book of *life*. (LK 10:20; REV 21:27)

When We Are Born-Again, The Old Man In Us Is Crucified With Christ

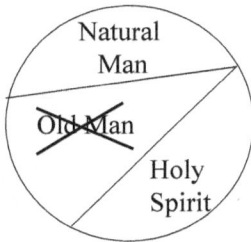

When we are "born-again", we are not only "saved" from the death sentence, but also delivered from the power of sin, itself. As mentioned in the last chapter, we are no longer in bondage to serve sin. We are set free to seek the kingdom of God and His righteousness. The "old man" in us that made us slaves to sin – that caused us to enjoy sinning – that convinced us that there was nothing wrong with what we were doing – is crucified with Christ (RO 6:6). God, sending His Holy Spirit to dwell within us, gives us the power to overcome the temptation and attraction of sin and instead to produce pure "fruit". "For when ye were servants of sin, ye were free from righteousness. What fruit had ye then in those things whereof ye are now ashamed? For the end of those things is death. But now being made free from sin, and become servants of God, ye have your fruit unto holiness, and the end everlasting life." (RO 6:20-22). "...greater is He that is in you, than he that is in the world." (1JN 4:4). That doesn't mean that we never sin – because our natural man is still alive in us. It means, however, that when we sin the Holy Spirit is faithful to convict us – so that we want to tell God we're sorry for it. And then because of Christ's sacrifice for our sin, He (can now be and) is faithful and just to forgive our sins and to cleanse us from all unrighteousness (1JN 1:9).

There was a missionary who was translating the Bible into a foreign language. He was struggling over the word for "believe". One day a *runner* brought a message to the missionary's camp. He was totally exhausted, found a hammock nearby and collapsed into it. He uttered a phrase that expressed simultaneously his weariness and his contentment at finding a delightful place to relax. They were words that the missionary had never heard before so he asked one of the natives to explain them. It turned out that the runner was saying that he was at the end of himself and was therefore resting all his weight in the hammock. The missionary then realized that these words correctly described what it meant to believe. To believe accurately means that we must first admit that we are sinners and can't help save ourselves – we're at the end of ourselves. Then we must turn from our sin and cast ourselves totally and unreservedly on Christ for salvation.

Faith is simply taking God at His word...

remember...

HE 11:1 - *"Now faith is the substance of things hoped for, the evidence of things not seen."*
Every morning, while driving to work, I come to a circle. Somewhere around that circle, during every season, at about the same time every morning, I will usually see the sun. There are times, however, that there are so many clouds in the sky that the sun is blocked from my view - but I know it's still there.

There will be times in your life as a Christian when troubles, trials, the stress of a situation, a prayer that goes unanswered for a long time, or even the injustice you see around you, block your clear view of Christ. Be assured, He is still there (HE 5:13) and He is always working things together for the good of those who love Him (RO8:28). At those times, He is still faithfully waiting to commune with us.

Here's the way to spell FAITH....

F_ORSAKING_
A_LL_
I_
T_RUST_
H_IM_

Salvation is like the young woman who was brought before the judge for sentencing after committing a crime. The judge issued the verdict after hearing all the evidence. He found her guilty and sentenced her to death – because the crime was deserving of the death sentence. The judge, however, cared very much for this woman because she was his daughter. So he pronounced the sentence but also pronounced that he would trade places with the woman and would suffer the penalty for her – she was spared because the judge accepted the sentence of death for her. The judge was executed for his daughter. Justice was accomplished but the judge showed the young woman great mercy. Similarly, at the cross when Christ was crucified for you and me, justice and mercy "embraced" and we were set free from the death sentence; while God, in the form of His Son, accepted the just punishment.

It's also like the story of the Wizard of Oz. Dorothy is caught in a great tornado and is hurled round and round – tossed to and fro. She is dropped into the land of Oz. That whirlwind is like the "roar of the crowd" on our life and we are delivered into a world where "self" is king and selfishness is the way of life. If we listen to our heart (the Tin man wanted a heart), and our mind (the scarecrow wanted a brain), and if we act courageously without concern for what the world might think (the lion wanted courage) like Dorothy, we sense that this place is not our final home. We try every way we can, like Dorothy, to get back to our real home.

We think we need to do something difficult – so we make "pilgrimages" to various places in our life - that could be like going to see the wizard of Oz. We might work hard at doing good deeds or trying different religions, or traveling to various scenic areas. We might make our family or education or material possessions our Oz. Just like the wizard who told Dorothy she would have to do this extraordinary feat of killing the wicked witch to get home, we listen to the "roar of the crowd" to run the race of life and finish well. Just like Dorothy, however, in the end the wizard is found out to be a fraud – who had no extraordinary powers to get her home.

Finally the good angel tells Dorothy that she had the power within herself to go home anytime she wanted to. She had the special "ruby" (red like the blood of Christ) shoes. So she begins to click her heels together and says, "There's no place like home, there's no place like home." And we too already have the power to make Heaven our home for life: God has provided the sacrifice of Christ on the cross and His resurrection from the dead. And "if you shall confess with your mouth the Lord Jesus and shall believe in your heart that God has raised Him from the dead, you shall be saved (RO 10:9).

Jesus said, "I am the way, the truth, and the life. No one goes unto the Father but by me." (JN 14:6).

Here's another illustration of what it means to "receive" Jesus Christ or "to believe on His name": Suppose you go to a doctor for an examination and he says that you have what was formerly a fatal disease. He tells you that medical science has discovered a drug that can cure you. It doesn't matter that you think he's a great physician or that his diagnosis is accurate or even that the medication is the best. You must TAKE THE MEDICATION to get better. If you don't, you'll die. Similarly, you must personally receive the Lord Jesus Christ. He's the only remedy for your sins.

Suppose you're brought to a hospital for emergency treatment. You don't know the doctor who's going to treat you but as he examines and talks with you, you're convinced he knows his business. You would probably say, "I want you to be my doctor and take care of me." That's how you "receive" Christ and are saved. When you hear the Gospel, you say to the Lord, "I want you to be my Savior."

Jesus is the forerunner of eternal life for us. He ran a race that only He could run. The Judge had already pronounced all the rest of us "losers" because of sin. That race took Him through the mud, dust, rocks, and thorns…and through the cross of Calvary. He sacrificed Himself for us so we could qualify for the race of eternal life. He was declared the Victor when He rose from the dead. When we receive Him, God makes all that Christ did become ours. "It is of him (i.e. God) that ye are in Christ." (1COR 1:30).

remember...

When we repent of our sins, and receive Jesus Christ and His sacrifice on the cross for forgiveness of our sins, then we are born - not of man or of the will of the flesh - but born of God. We are called "born-again".(John 1:12-13) We are said to be "born of the Spirit". (John 3:8) The Holy Spirit takes up residence within our spirit. We are "new creations" because the Holy Spirit makes us into someone who has never existed before. We used to be unique creations, but now we are a brand new member of God's family. Just like the blood is common that flows in the veins of members of the same physical family, likewise the Holy Spirit is common in all Christians and makes us members of God's family. Also see the following scriptures about being "born-again": Romans 3:23; 5:12;5:8;6:23;10:13;10:9-11

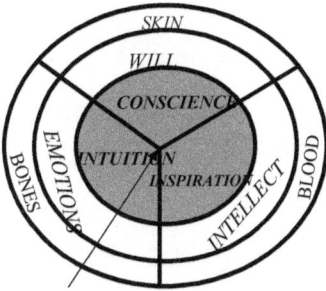

Here's where the Holy Spirit lives in us. Jesus said that the Spirit would lead us into all truth. To do that, He uses our Studying the Word of God, Prayer, Worship, Fellowship, Service, as well as our Trials/Tribulations.

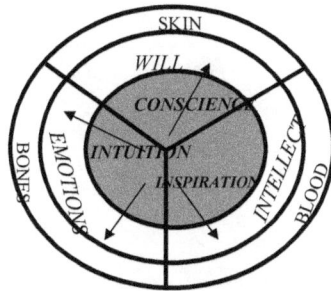

The Holy Spirit works to change us into Christ's image by working especially in our spirit and soul. Although all Christians have the Spirit - and are thereby part of God's family - the Holy Spirit doesn't have all of us. The natural man in us competes with the Spirit and must be reduced to zero.

When we are born-again, we have a "personal" relationship to Jesus Christ – because we have received Him and become children of God (JN 1:12). We also have a personal relationship to others who have received Jesus. We have the same heavenly Father. Jesus has become not only our Savior and Lord, but also our Brother and a Friend that sticks closer than a brother (PR 18:24). Before receiving Christ in this way, we all fell short of God's expectations – whether we were "good" or "bad" in the world's eyes. We may have been faithful to the ritual of attending church services – or even doing many benevolent works that required great sacrifice. These, however, are not recognized by God as satisfying the penalty for sin and do not bring us into a personal relationship with Christ. They also do not provide the "peace of God that passes understanding" like this personal relationship does. (PH 4:7)

As in any relationship, the two who are related make time to keep themselves close. God took the initiative in drawing us to Himself by making Jesus the sacrifice for our sins. Now Jesus takes the initiative in nurturing our new relationship with Him. He says, "Come unto me all those who labor and are heavy laden, and I will give you rest. Take my yoke upon you and learn of me for I am meek and lowly of heart; and you shall find rest unto your souls." (MT 11:28-29) The primary ways to have intimacy with God, and keep this personal relationship current and vibrant are prayer, worship, study of God's Word – the Bible, fellowship with other born-again believers, and surrendering to God for service.

Chapter 3

Entering The Gymnasium
"The Kingdom of God"

Lenny had entered the kingdom of God that day he received Jesus Christ into his heart. The invisible kingdom within him had taken hold. The experience of his dream was so powerful that after entering the kingdom of God, Lenny asked everyone to call him "Liv". If the Lord called him that name, then he felt he should use it himself. So whenever he signed his name, it was always, Liv Livright.

But Lenny was a stubborn man and he knew very little about the importance of fellowship with other believers in the visible kingdom. He had been a "good" Catholic all his life and he wanted to continue attending that church. Another neighbor, seeing Lenny's interest in "religious" things invited him to become part of the Knights of Columbus – but that didn't satisfy. He then invited him to become a part of the Rosary Society – but that too fell short of what his spirit was searching for.

Two incidents during mass convinced Lenny that he needed to change churches. One day the priest came off the altar and started to preach as he walked up the center aisle. He said, "Some people are destroying everything that is good and holy today. Take, for example, the confessional. They think that instead of confessing sins to a priest, they can just kneel down in their own homes and confess them to God. And they think God will forgive them if they do just that." Well Lenny believed that since he had found the source of his salvation by reading the Bible, it was something he should keep doing. He read the Bible as he commuted to work on a chartered bus. And he had already read by now in the first letter of John, chapter 1 and verse 9, "If we confess our sins, he is faithful and just to forgive us our sins and cleanse us from all unrighteousness." He knew that it was Christ's blood that provided cleansing from sin – not how many prayers we say or whether we tell a priest or not. Lenny thought, "This priest must not be reading his Bible."

The other incident happened on All Souls Day. That's when Catholics pray for the souls of those who have died before them. All the seats in the rear of the church were filled so Lenny forced himself to get up close. The priest (a different one than above) seemed to have the biggest, darkest rings around his eyes. He looked out at that large congregation and said, "Do you really think that you're good enough to go directly to heaven. You know you're not good enough. There needs to be a place where you can pay for your sins and suffer before you go to heaven. That place is Purgatory. We need to pray for the souls there because some day it might be you." Well Lenny said there's something wrong here. Isn't this priest reading his Bible either? In the letter of Paul to the Ephesians, Chapter 2 and verse 8 and 9 it says, "For grace are ye saved through faith; and that not of yourselves: it is the gift of God: Not of works lest any man should boast." He knew that God bestowed salvation immediately because of Christ. Even Jesus told the thief on the cross that "today you shall be with me in paradise".

Lenny knew he had to leave this church and began looking for another Catholic church. One day, however, when Lenny and his family were with the Rightraks, Esther asked him if he would come to church with them next Sunday. They went to a nondenominational church and Lenny was afraid to go to a non-Catholic church. But because of their love for Lenny, he wouldn't refuse them and agreed to go. That Sunday service turned out to be like getting to heaven itself. Lenny's spirit found peace and joy with other believers and hearing the Word of God being taught and preached. They sang a song that day that Lenny's never forgotten: "There's a new name written down in glory and it's mine!" He was so overjoyed at finding a real "home" that he put all of five dollars in the collection that day. Before that, it was always quarters. And though he would learn about disciplining himself and being a good steward of his money later on, the Lord knew Lenny was trying to say "Thank you, Lord, for searching for and finding this lost sheep. Thank you for leading me to a place where I can grow and become what you want me to be!"

Entering the Gymnasium – Biblical Principles and Application

Jesus went on to explain to Nicodemas more about this being born again or literally born from above. He said, "Except a man be born of water (i.e. physical birth) and the Spirit (i.e. spiritual birth from God), he cannot enter the kingdom of God." (JN 3: 3-5).

To get on the real race track means we need to enter the gymnasium where the event takes place. The Bible calls this place the "kingdom of God". Jesus tells us that the entrance requirements – the key to the gym – involve not only having our physical birth, but also the spiritual birth from God that we discussed in the last chapter. What, however, is this kingdom like? Where is it located?

The "kingdom of God" refers to the spiritual rule of God in the hearts of His people through Jesus Christ. There is the unseen "kingdom" within each believer. In LK 17:20-21, Jesus says, "...the kingdom of God is within you." And RO 14:17 says, "The kingdom of God is righteousness, peace and joy in the Holy Ghost." This kingdom of God is within each Christian person.

There is also the kingdom of God that is visible, consisting of all the places where Christians take their "stand" for Christ (EPH 6:11, 13, 14). When Adam and Eve sinned, not only did man lose his spiritual life and come under the bondage of sin, but also in a spiritual sense God "lost" the earth. He began the work to recover the earth with Abraham and down through the children of Israel to Christ. Through Christ, that recovery continues through those who receive Him. Wherever a Christian "stands" for Christ, part of the world is recovered for God. Today this "kingdom" is in many pieces all over the world. God has His men and women in China, Brazil, Germany, Russia, and almost every other country of the world. They are "holding ground" for Him in the workplace, in their homes, in political arenas, in the classrooms, in religious and social organizations. One day Christ will deliver to His Father all the kingdoms of this world – wherever principalities, powers, and hierarchies of influence in the world compete with Christ for the souls of man. REV 11:15 says, "The kingdoms of this world have become the kingdoms of our God and his Christ. And he shall rule for ever and ever."

1 COR 3: 9 calls this visible kingdom "God's building". It is also referred to as the Church or the Body of Christ (1COR 12:20, 27; EPH 1:22-23). The invisible kingdom within each believer is to be a microcosm of the visible kingdom. Progress toward the finish line in this "seen" kingdom depends very much upon the believers' personal progress. You can see the similarities and relationship between them by considering their major characteristics: Growth, Sanctification, Grace and Forgiveness, Relationship, Trials and Tribulations, Discipline, Spiritual Warfare, and Good Stewardship.

Growth

- THE INVISIBLE KINGDOM - BELIEVERS' PERSONAL GROWTH – We call a Christian's personal growth becoming spiritually mature, which God measures as "Christlikeness". To be like Christ is the goal of the Christian life. EPH 4:13 says, "Till we all come in the unity of the faith, and of the knowledge of the Son of God, unto a perfect man, unto the measure of the stature of the fullness of Christ. PH 3:8-13 speaks of knowing Christ in an intimate way in order to become like Him. " ...I count all things but loss for the excellency of the knowledge of Christ Jesus my Lord: for whom I have suffered the loss of all things, and do count them but dung, that I may win Christ...That I may know him, and the power of his resurrection, and the fellowship of his sufferings, being made conformable unto his death...Brethren, I count not myself to have apprehended: but this one thing I do, forgetting those things that are behind, and reaching forth unto those things that are before, I press toward the mark for the prize of the high calling of God in Christ Jesus." This is a picture of the Christian who desires to win the prize of the Christian life – to be like Christ.
- THE VISIBLE KINGDOM – GROWTH OF THE CHURCH – The Apostle Peter shows us how the growth of individual Christians causes the Church to grow also. When we desire to grow by "drinking in" the truth of God's Word, we are built into a building that, he says, is made up of "lively stones" (i.e. stones that are living and growing). Here's how he expresses that thought, "...laying aside all malice, and all guile, and hypocrisies, and envies, and all evil speaking, as newborn babes, desire the sincere milk of the word, that you may grow thereby...you

also as lively stones, are built up (into) a spiritual house, a holy priesthood, to offer up spiritual sacrifices, acceptable to God by Jesus Christ." (1 PE 2: 1-5)

EPH 4:16 adds additional insight by showing that the Body of Christ grows as each of its members (i.e. believers) do their individual work and "touch" the lives of other believers. The word "joint" in Greek could actually be translated "touch". "...Christ: from whom the whole body (is) fitly joined together and compacted by that which every joint supplies, according to the effectual working in the measure of every part, makes increase of the body unto the edifying of itself in love."

Sanctification

- THE INVISIBLE KINGDOM – PERSONAL SANCTIFICATION. The word "sanctification" means separation from the world and separation unto God. It's holiness. It's dying and living. It's reckoning ourselves to be dead to sin and alive to God. Another word for it might be "consecration". RO 6:11-13 says, " Likewise reckon...yourselves to be dead indeed unto sin, but alive unto God through Jesus Christ our Lord. Let not sin reign in your mortal body, that you should obey it in the lusts thereof. Neither yield your members as instruments of unrighteousness unto sin: but yield yourselves unto God as those that are alive from the dead, and your members as instruments of righteousness unto God."

Jesus mentions in JN 14:21-23 that those who truly love Him will keep His commandments – that's a measure of our true love for Him. He says further, "If a man loves me, he will keep my words: and my Father will love him, and we will come unto him and make our abode (i.e. home) with him." In future chapters we will address this aspect of "purity" by allowing Christ to take us on an incredible journey through our hearts. Though God's Holy Spirit takes up residence in any heart that truly repents and receives Christ, as we mature in Christ we want our heart to become a home that honors His name.

38 - Run The Race of Life – The Real Way

* Adapted from "Commitment to a Local Expression of The Body of Christ", Larry Tomczak & C.J. Mahaney, 1978

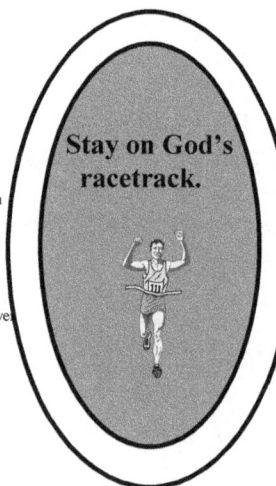

Kingdom of the World	*Kingdom of God*
Satan - The god of this world (2COR 4:4)	Jesus is Lord! (PH 2:11)

Stay on God's racetrack.

Kingdom of the World	Kingdom of God
• Seeing is believing	• Believing is seeing (JN 20:29)
• Wise	• Fool (1COR 3:18)
• Save your life	• Lose your life (MT 16:25)
• First	• Last (MK 9:35)
• Great	• Least (MK 10:43)
• Ruler	• Servant (MK 10:43)
• Exalted	• Humble Yourself (LK 14:11)
• Look to your own interests	• Look to others' interests. Count others better than self (PH 2:3)
• Get much	• Give much (LK 6:38)
• Make your good deeds known	• Keep your good deeds secret (MT 6:3)
• Love is feeling & conditional	• Love is commitment & unconditional (JN 15:12-13)
• Love grows cold	• Love never fails (1COR 13:8)
• Hate your enemies	• Love your enemies (MT 5:44)
• Retaliate	• Forgive (COL 3:13)
• Human might and human power	• Not by might/power but by my Spirit (ZECH 3:6)
• Eat, drink, and be merry	• Man doesn't live by bread alone(MT 4:4)
• It is impossible	• Everything is possible (MK 9:23)
• Check your stars	• Search the scriptures (JN 5:39)
• Bible was written by man	• Bible inspired by God (2TI 3:16)
• Bible is outdated	• My words shall never pass away (MT 24:35)
• Jesus was a good man	• Jesus is Lord! (PH 2:11)
• Jesus is dead	• Jesus Christ the same yesterday, today, and forever! (HE 13:8)
• Jesus is not coming again	• I will come again and take you (JN 14:3)

- **THE VISIBLE KINGDOM - SANCTIFICATION OF THE CHURCH.** Jesus prayed to His heavenly Father in JN 17:15-17, "I pray not that thou should take them out of the world, but that thou should keep them from the evil. They are not of the world, even as I am not of the world. Sanctify them by thy truth: thy word is truth." And then He says that as the Father sent Him into the world, He has sent us into the world. He says that He was sanctifying Himself so that we could be sanctified as we see the truth and emulate Him. He then prays that the individual Christians would be one as He and our Father are one (verse 21). As Christians separate themselves from the world and unto God, they will be drawn together in a holy union that will testify to the world that Christ is who He said He was. "…that they also may be one in us: that the world might believe that you sent me." (Verse 21) As individual Christians grow in holiness, the church, the visible kingdom of God, will be "in the world but not of the world." (JN 15:19)

Grace and Forgiveness

- THE INVISIBLE KINGDOM – PERSONAL GRACE & FORGIVENESS – Grace is a word that means "unmerited favor". It means getting much more than you deserve to get. A good way to remember its meaning is to use the letters in GRACE this way: Gods Riches At Christ's Expense. It is, after all, God's grace that extends salvation to everyone. "By grace are you saved through faith; and that not of yourselves: it is the gift of God: Not of works, lest any man boast." (EPH 2:8-9). It is closely connected with Christians extending forgiveness. EPH 4:32 says, "Be...kind one to another, tenderhearted, forgiving one another, even as God for Christ's sake hath forgiven you." Also see EPH 2:7.

- THE VISIBLE KINGDOM - GRACE & FORGIVENESS IN THE CHURCH. 1PE 1:2 shows us that this quality is to be manifested by the church also – especially as it is extended to those who are still under the yoke of sin as we all once were. Extend grace to those who are perhaps losing the battle with the enemy of their soul – those who are struggling to find their way home "...Grace be unto you, and peace, be multiplied. Blessed be God and Father of our Lord Jesus Christ, which according to his abundant mercy hath begotten us again unto a lively hope by the resurrection of Jesus from the dead, To an inheritance incorruptible, and undefiled, and that fadeth not away, reserved in heaven for you, Who are kept by the power of God through faith unto salvation..."

Jesus told a parable that demonstrates for us how He wants both individual believers and the church to extend this grace and forgiveness. It's called THE PARABLE OF PRODICAL SON (LK 15:11-32). A son tells his father that he wants his rightful inheritance right away. He leaves his father and brother and squanders all of his father's money on harlots and fast living. When he hits bottom and has absolutely nothing to eat, he decides that he'd be better off working as a hired hand with his father. He decides that when he returns he will confess his sin to his father and beg him to treat him as a hired hand since he wasn't worthy to be his son any longer. The father had everyday peered far and long into the horizon with the hope of possibly catching a glimpse of his long lost son returning home. And one day, he sees his son a long way off. This wonderful father had compassion on his son and ran to meet him, embracing him before his son even uttered a single word. When the son confessed his unworthiness, his father put a ring on his son's hand and ordered his servant to kill the fatted calf for a celebration. "For this my son was dead, and is alive again; he was lost, and is found." (verse 24).

Relationship

- THE INVISIBLE KINGDOM – OUR PERSONAL RELATIONSHIP WITH GOD AND EACH OTHER. This is the work of the cross. Our relationship with God, our Father, was broken because of our being in bondage to sin. Christ was crucified to pay the penalty for sin (i.e. death) and to restore us to our heavenly Father. As individual believers, the way we believe inwardly is the way we behave outwardly. Our inner attitudes about relating to God and others are manifested in our outward behavior. It's manifested, for example, in how we serve God and our brothers and sisters in Christ. It is manifested in how we worship God – wholeheartedly or half-hearted. It is manifested in our fellowship with God through our prayer life and with other believers through sharing our lives with them. Inwardly, we study the Bible and develop a disciplined prayer life to get to know Christ better; or perhaps we neglect these things.

  Jesus encourages us to nourish our relationships – especially with Him and our Father in LK 12. "The life is more than meat and the body is more than raiment...And seek not ye what ye shall eat, or what ye shall drink, neither be ye of doubtful mind. For all these things do the nations of the world seek after: and your Father knows that ye have need of these things. But rather seek ye the kingdom of God; and all these things shall be added unto you...for where your treasure is, there will your heart be also." (Verses 22-34).

- THE VISIBLE KINGDOM – RELATIONSHIP OF THE CHURCH. All of these, become the way the church relates to its members and the world around it. As members grow closer to our heavenly Father, He directs them to relate to those who are beyond the kingdom's borders – to bring them into His kingdom. Remember the great compassion of Jesus when He looked upon the crowds who came to hear Him speak (e.g. MT 14:14-21). Once when He was going into all the cities teaching and preaching the Gospel (i.e. good news of God's love through Christ) and healing the sick, He was moved with compassion because they were like weak sheep without a shepherd. He said, "The harvest truly is plenteous, but the laborers are few; Pray ye therefore the Lord of the harvest, that he will send forth laborers into his harvest." (MT 9:37-38).

So as we nurture our relationship with God, He will move us in the visible kingdom to have compassion for others in the kingdom and those in the world "outside". The world would then know that the Father sent His Son into the world to have compassion on sinners. (JN 17:21). On the other hand, if we do not nurture our relationship with Him, and not allow Him to move us with His love for all people, then the world "outside" will not be seeing Christ as He really is but rather some caricature of the risen Christ. They may then decide that the Church, God's visible kingdom, is no more than some social club or fraternity.

Trials and Tribulation

- THE INVISIBLE KINGDOM – PERSONAL TRIALS AND TRIBULATION. This is the reality of the cross. In JN 16:33 Jesus said, "These things I have spoken unto you, that in me ye might have peace. In the world ye shall have tribulation: but be of good cheer; I have overcome the world." Suffering is a part of the Christian life. We, however, have an advantage over those who do not have Christ. He goes with us in every trial. He never leaves us forsaken. In addition, He comforts us. He then uses us to comfort others with the same comfort He used to comfort us (2COR 1:4). According to 1PE 1:7, the trying of our faith is more precious than gold tried in the fire – The goldsmith sees his face and the gold is purified – God sees Christ's image in us and His work is complete. Peter says, "That the trying of your faith, being more precious than of gold that perisheth, though it be tried, might be found unto praise and honor and glory at the appearing of Jesus Christ..."
- THE VISIBLE KINGDOM – PERSECUTION OF THE CHURCH. I am amazed sometimes at how many enemies we Christians seem to have for what appears to be no reason at all. However, when we take our

"stand" in the kingdom for what God stands for; and when we live "in the world but not of it", there's little doubt about why we upset those whose values and behaviors are so contrary to our own. This can be seen quite visibly by the persecution received by churches in various countries for taking their stand for Christ there. These countries include China, North Korea, Vietnam, Sudan, Pakistan, Kuwait, and Saudi Arabia. Even this is used by our Lord to draw many to Himself by the faith, courage, and endurance of those who suffer "the loss of all things" for "the excellency of knowing Christ."

Discipline

- THE INVISIBLE KINGDOM – PERSONAL DISCIPLINE. The word "discipline" comes from the word "disciple", which means "learner". Jesus said that there were two ways that man could go. He encouraged us to go by way of the narrow gate, "for wide is the gate, and broad is the way that leads to destruction." He said that the gate that leads to life is narrow (MT 7: 13-14). He also says, "If any man would come after me (i.e. be my disciple), let him deny himself, take up his cross daily, and follow me." (LK 9:23). Jesus said, "...whosoever of you that forsaketh not all that he hath, he cannot be my disciple." (LK 14:33). "If you continue in my word, then are ye my disciples in deed." (JN 8:31).

  The life of Christ's disciples is boundless in terms of accomplishment because we can do all things through Christ that strengthens us. At the same time, it has boundaries in our beliefs, values, and behaviors. The track of the Christian race is "marked" and we follow the boundary markers that help keep us "on course". So Paul says, "I press toward the mark..." (PH 3:14). "...and let us run with patience the race that is set before us..." (HE12:1).

  The Christian life is marked by self-denial, sacrifice, discipline and patient endurance. It is marked by waiting upon the Lord and having Him renew our strength to keep running well (IS 40:31). It is marked by serving others. Christ demonstrated this so vividly in His ministry here on earth (e.g. JN 13:13-14). It is marked by the "new commandment" He gave us "to love one another as I have loved you...By this shall all men know that ye are my disciples, if ye love one another." (JN 13:34-35). This love requires giving our lives for one another. Here's some of the ways we can learn to love others:

- Learn to listen.
- Learn to "touch". Touch people not only physically, but also with a card, a phone call, a visit, a benevolence, etc.
- Learn to let go and let God lead.
- Learn how to tell others what's inside.
- Learn to feel (i.e. empathize). Learn to cry together and relinquish the "spotlight" to someone else.

- THE VISIBLE KINGDOM – DISCIPLINE OF THE CHURCH. As Christians surrender to the Lord's discipline work, as members individually, the church is then characterized as a self-sacrificing organism – a body that will sacrifice its time, talents, and treasure to save the lost and to build itself up in love. Just as little parts of a powerful car engine are critical to keep it running well (like a wire that goes to the spark plug) every member of the visible kingdom of God is important. Speaking in REV 2:19 to the church in Thyatira, Jesus said, "I know thy works, and charity, and service, and faith, and thy patience,...." Paul teaches us as a church to be disciplined about the gifts God has bestowed on us. In 1 COR 12:7, we learn that these gifts are not given just to benefit those who receive them. They are given to individuals to benefit and serve the church (i.e. all the believers that the Lord sets in that church). "For as we have many members in one body, and all members have not the same office: So we, being many, are one body in Christ, and every one members one of another. Having then gifts differing according to the grace that is given us, whether prophecy, let us prophesy according to the proportion of faith; or ministry, let us wait on our ministering...Let love be (sincere)...Be kindly affectioned one to another...distributing to the necessity of the saints..." (RO 12:4-13).

EPH 4:16 demonstrates how the individual "touches" of members cause the church to be built up in love into the image of Christ. In the power of that great love, the church then reaches out to fulfill the Great Commission of Christ to "make disciples of all nations." (MT 28:19).

On the other hand, the failure of one member to pray could cause loss of power. Another who fails to give his testimony may mean that someone doesn't hear the good news of Jesus Christ. Another who neglects God's urging to support a church project with his finances could result in a shortfall in missions or evangelism.

Spiritual Warfare

*   THE INVISIBLE KINGDOM – PERSONAL SPIRITUAL WARFARE. We have already discussed this warfare in each Christian's life. We fight "not against flesh and blood but against principalities and powers in high places". (EPH 6:12). We battle against the world (JA 4:14), the flesh (JA 4: 3), and the devil (JA 4: 7). 1JN 2:16 says, "the lust of the eyes, lust of the flesh, and pride of life are not of the father but of the world." Where is the battle?

    There are two personal battlefields: One is within us and the other is out in the world. RO13:12 tells us that we need to put away envy, strife, guilt, doubt, fear, enmity between us and our brothers and sisters in Christ. We need to put off the works of "darkness" and put on the "armor of light". EPH 6: 11-18 explains how we need to combat the battle that rages within: "Put on the whole armor of God, that ye may be able to stand against the wiles of the devil...take unto you the whole armor of God, that ye may be able to stand in the evil day, and having done all to stand. Stand, therefore, having your loins girt about with truth, and having on the breastplate of righteousness; And your feet shod with the preparation of the gospel of peace; Above all, taking the shield of faith, wherewith ye shall be able to quench all the fiery darts of the wicked. And take the helmet of salvation, and the sword of the Spirit, which is the word of God: Praying always with all perseverance and supplication in the spirit, and watching thereunto...for all the saints."

    Out in the world, outside the kingdom of God, people are in a battle for their souls. They are our potential comrades and brothers in this fight, and are losing the battle. We are God's ambassadors (EPH 6:20; 2COR 5:20) to bring the message of salvation to them. REV 12:11 tells us that we need to use "the blood of the Lamb and the word of our testimony" to defeat the devil. We need to tell them about Jesus' shed blood for them and tell them how we ourselves came to Christ.

- THE VISIBLE KINGDOM - SPIRITUAL WARFARE OF THE CHURCH. In MT 16:18, Jesus says that upon the "rock" of His being the Christ, Son of the living God, He would build His Church. Furthermore, " the gates of hell shall not prevail against it". It is the picture of an attacking church that knocks down the gates of hell with its prisoners under the bondage of sin.

  The Church, too, has an enemy within. In evaluating the churches in REV 2:13, Jesus says of the church at Pergamos, "I know thy works, and where thou dwellest, even where Satan's seat is. The PARABLE OF THE MUSTARD SEED in LK 13: 18-19 speaks of the kingdom of God being like "a grain of mustard seed, which a man took and cast into his garden; and it grew, and (became) a great tree; and the fowls of the air lodged in the branches of it." Jesus continued to say that the kingdom of God is "like leaven, which a woman took and hid in three measures of meal, till the whole was leavened." LK 13:20-21. The "birds" that lodged in the branches are symbolic of the birds that ate the seed (the word sowed into peoples' hearts) in the PARABLE OF THE SOWER (MT 13:3-23). Verse 19 tells us that the birds that take away the seed represent "that wicked one" (i.e. Satan). He has lodged in the Church. The "leaven" represents Satan's deceit.

Stewardship

- THE INVISIBLE KINGDOM – PERSONAL STEWARDSHIP. Each Christian is to use the resources (time, talents, money, information) God has given him to be productive. MT 25:14-30 is the PARABLE OF THE TALENTS. Jesus tells how the "kingdom of heaven" is like a man travelling into a far country who gives his goods to his servants according to their abilities. They are to manage his business while he's gone. After a long time, the owner returns and begins to "reckon" with his servants. Those who increased the money entrusted to them were rewarded. They were told, "Well done thou good and faithful servant: thou hast been faithful over a few things. I will make thee ruler over many things: enter into the joy of thy lord." (Verses 21, 23). There was one servant, however, who did not gain anything with his lord's money. That servant was cast into outer darkness where there is "weeping and gnashing of teeth." (Verse 30). WE NEED TO BE A CHANNEL NOT A CUP with the personal resources our Lord entrusts to us.

One special note here before going on. There is another "kingdom" which Jesus spoke about and we quoted it just above – it's the "kingdom of heaven". This is the kingdom beyond – the kingdom to come. Note that in the PARABLE OF THE TALENTS it's about the owner leaving and then returning. One day, when Christ returns and sets up His kingdom on earth, the "kingdom of God" and the "kingdom of heaven" will be the same. Here are some scriptures that speak of this coming kingdom of heaven:

- DAN 2:44   "In those days, the Son of God will set up a kingdom."
- MT 17:2 On the mount of transfiguration Jesus shows Peter, James, and John the coming King in His glory – and we shall return with Him and be like Him – DAN 12:3
- LK 22:27-30 "And I bestow upon you a kingdom, just as my Father bestowed one upon me. That you might eat and drink at my table in my kingdom, and sit on thrones judging the 12 tribes of Israel."
- JN 18:36 "My kingdom is not of this world."
- PH2:10 "At the name of Jesus every knee shall bow and every tongue confess to the glory of God the Father."
- REV 11:15 "The kingdoms of this world have become the kingdoms of our God and his Christ; and he shall reign for ever and ever."

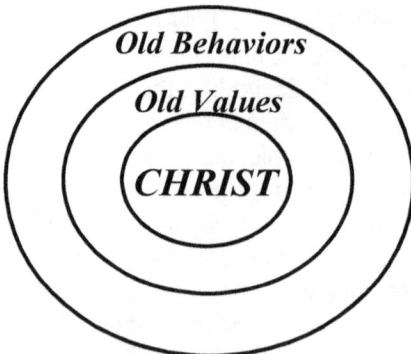

Old Behaviors
Old Values
CHRIST

- THE VISIBLE KINGDOM -

GOOD STEWARDSHIP OF THE CHURCH. The church becomes a channel to the missionaries to seek the lost and preach the gospel. It becomes a channel to the sick, those in nursing homes and hospitals. It becomes a channel to the needy, the broken hearted, the fatherless, the widow, the prisoners, and the marriages in crisis. The church is a channel to each of its members to pray, serve, prefer, love, admonish, forgive, warn, restore gently, bear with, and fellowship with one another. We also bear each others' burdens. The church becomes a good steward of its time, talents, and treasure. ACTS 2: 45 and ACTS 4:35 show us that there should be no lack in the church. And as we work together we can evangelize the whole world (JN 17:21).

So, when we are born-again, we enter this kingdom of God – both the visible and invisible one. We begin very soon after entering to understand that Christ must be in the center of our world view not self. We realize that it is not *my* will but *His* will that matters most. In a way, this is a new start in our Christian race.

We begin to learn how to run for our life God's way – how to live this new life. Even though we realize Christ must be the "hub" around which our life revolves, the old values and behaviors that we learned from the roar of the crowd are still with us. The natural man is alive in us and competes with Christ in us. It takes time for the old values and behaviors to be

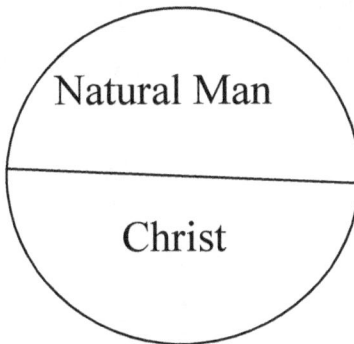

The Old Man Has Been Crucified With Christ (Ro 6:6) But The Natural Man Still Competes With Christ

Us After We Are Born Again

changed. This is shown clearly in Acts 10: 9-16 when Peter, after our Lord's resurrection and ascension, has a dream on the rooftop of one called Simon the tanner. In his dream a blanket is lowered from Heaven with many unclean animals aboard. The Lord tells Peter to "kill and eat". But Peter – now a born again Christian – says, "No, Lord, since I've been a child no unclean meat has ever touched my lips." Three times the Lord gives the same command and Peter repeats his answer. Peter had learned that eating what were considered unclean meats was wrong.   He didn't understand Christ's admonishment to the Pharisees that it is not what enters the man that is sin but what comes out of the man that is sin.

Another illustration of how the old values stick with us when we come to Christ, is in Luke 5: 36-39. Here the Lord tells us that no man puts new wine in old wineskins – because the old wineskin doesn't stretch and the old wineskin will break and the wine will spill on the ground. But Jesus said that new wine is put in new wineskins so both can be preserved. At this point He was teaching us that we must maintain a new wineskin "heart" so He can pour new truth into us. But then He makes a remarkable statement – He says, "But no one who's tasted the old, immediately desires the new because the old tastes better." In other words, no one immediately accepts new truth – it's hard to change! The old values stick with us.

When Christians lean more on their natural instincts and abilities (i.e. the natural man) rather than on Christ's gifts and His strength, we call that person a "carnal Christian". He's depending more on the "flesh" than on Christ. The process of changing those old values in the Christian is normally called discipleship. What's needed is a RO12: 2 transformation, "Be not conformed to this world, but be ye transformed by the renewing of your mind that you may prove what is that perfect, acceptable will of God

Chapter 4

The Discipline To Win
The Transformation

The days and early years after Liv received Jesus as Savior and Lord were mixed with baggage carried from the old life as well as exciting new experiences and lessons. Esther took responsibility for developing Liv into the disciple that God wanted him to be. One of the first experiences she gave him was giving his testimony to strangers. In those days, the Lord was moving in various churches through "lay witness missions" and "faith alive". Churches were inviting lay people to give their testimonies of how they had received Christ to people of their own congregations. Esther asked Liv to accompany her to a church in Maryland. To Liv, it was like going into battle again – only this time he was on a mission for the Lord. About 12-15 people from different parts of the country, different denominations, and different levels of Christian maturity came together at the church. The team seemed to melt together into an elite spiritual fighting force as Liv, Esther, and the others raised their voices in praise to Jesus. They sang songs like "Alleluia", "Give Me Oil In My Lamp", "Your Name Is Wonderful", and "Seek Ye First The Kingdom Of God".

On Friday night in a church service several members gave their testimonies – not Liv or Esther. But they had a chance later in small groups to pray for the needs of people in this congregation. Liv was asked to pray for one lady's back problem. The prayer was mainly to thank Jesus for being present and for loving this woman – and He healed the woman, who later shared that in front of the congregation. Liv was also asked to lead a small coffee Bible study in a church member's home on Saturday afternoon and later that day he gave his testimony. Saturday afternoon, Liv heard

Esther's testimony. She kept everyone laughing and received many compliments afterward.

Later that day, everyone went to a very old landmark church to have a break. One of the older members of the team noticed a pump organ in the church and was permitted to play a song. She said her legs wouldn't be able to handle more than one. Everyone joined in singing and one by one, amazingly, they kept singing and she kept pumping. And soon Liv was in awe when he heard what seemed like a full choir of angels adding their voices with the team's. On Sunday morning, the leader of the mission gave his testimony and then asked if anyone wanted to receive Jesus. Liv was amazed at how many received Christ that day. When everyone had said their goodbye with many tears, Esther asked Liv to pray with her at the altar. She thanked God for doing His great work in peoples' lives and also gave back to Him all the compliments she had received.

After several lay witness missions, Liv accepted the invitation to be a leader. At one meeting alone, sixty people accepted his invitation to receive Christ. Giving his testimony became something Liv would do as he ran for his life God's way. Once when he was commuting on the charter bus back from work, he heard a man trying to convince a woman that there was no God. It was a crowded bus, very noisy with many talking, and Liv was standing so he couldn't join the conversation. But he knew God wanted him to say something to this woman – but where would she get off the bus? How could he discuss this with her? His heart pounded within him. He had to do it. Well, God planned for this woman to get off just one stop before Liv's. But as she ran across the street, the bus blocked Liv's view of her. After she had walked some distance, Liv ran after her calling to her to stop. She stopped and waited for him to speak. Liv began, "God wanted me to say..." And before he finished, she said, "I told God that if one more person stopped me and told me about the Lord, I would receive Jesus as my Savior." And so Liv prayed for her on the sidewalk, next to the parking lot – and a new name was written down in glory!

Other people, organizations, and churches would involve Liv in their activities. Though his heart was always in what he did for the Lord, he needed to learn better how to do it by the Holy Spirit and not in his own strength. It was hard for him to say "no" to anyone's request for help in ministry – learning that lesson would come later. He also was still someone who was afraid to admit ignorance and for a while felt very uncomfortable around authority figures like a pastor or elder in the church. He didn't have much close fellowship in those days because he felt that being self-reliant and sure of himself, as a Christian, was the way to be. He also knew very little about stewardship. Though he tithed his salary as soon as he saw it in scripture, he also saved very little because he believed that Christ would return right away.

A significant event occurred when Liv and his family were in Germany. A group of Army men and women wanted a small group Bible study. As just mentioned, sharing life with others in close communion and being accountable was not something Liv had experienced. Here's how God brought that about for this still rather stubborn Christian: He made several trips to the U.S. every year. Once on the return trip, Liv had two seats to himself and was so grateful to be able to stretch out. The stewardess was about to close the door, when another man jumped on the plane. His seat was next to Lenny. And soon they were sharing their Christian testimonies. He was a missionary to the soldiers and they shared each other's phone numbers and addresses. One day, Liv got a call from a sailor who had been at the missionary's meetings. He had told the sailor that he was sure Liv would love to host a Bible study for him and his friends.

This fellowship proved to last two years and showed Liv that the Lord was faithful and could use him in a teaching ministry – something that God would use throughout Liv's walk. People were saved through this Bible study. One lesbian in the Army, who kept very quiet for many of the Bible study meetings, eventually accepted Jesus as her Savior and Lord. Her life was transformed. She married and later had children and was teaching Bible studies herself. This home Bible study resulted in Liv co-leading a group of one hundred Christians who met on Sunday night for worship and prayer time. The group learned how to care for and be accountable to one another. For example, when one of the guys had missed Liv's meeting and also didn't show up for duty, the others went and found him "hung over" in his quarters. They nursed him with "coffee and prayer" back to his job and Liv's Bible study. At another time, Liv's daughter's gerbil had gotten loose and hid behind a wall in the apartment. She was frantic about losing her pet. At the risk of getting bitten, one of the soldiers stuck his hand in the wall and retrieved it. Some of these rough and tumble men also learned how to love and give themselves to Liv's two young children.

The Discipline to Win – Biblical Principles and Application

The Transformation

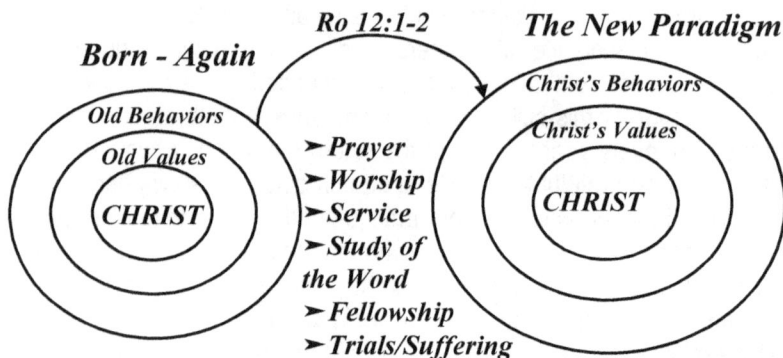

God is a real Person. He feels, He hurts, He wills, He thinks, He enjoys, He hates, etc. He can be known in varying degrees of intimacy. As we run for our life God's way, we must ask ourselves, "Do we really want to know Him?" The apostle Paul answered that question for himself. He said, "…and I count all things but loss for the excellency of the knowledge of Jesus my Lord…That I might know him, and the power of his resurrection, and the fellowship of his sufferings…" (PH 3:8,10). What's your answer? What's my answer? The truth is that as we desire and seek to know the Lord, we will embrace Christ's values and behaviors. We will be transformed from the values and behaviors that previously took precedence in our lives. "Draw nigh to God, and he will draw nigh to you." (JA 4:8). What is your greatest desire? Whatever that is will determine what you become and what you value most. Jesus said, "For where your treasure is, there your heart will be also." (MT 6:21).

God is always calling us to know Him better. In the garden, Adam and Eve hid themselves from God after sinning. God called to Adam, "Where art thou?" (GEN 3:9). Do you hear the loneliness in God's voice? Do you feel His broken heart? Over the centuries, God has continued to call man to Himself. The greatest demonstration of this was when He sent Christ to restore the broken relationship with us. Even after we receive Jesus, however, God keeps calling from the depths of His heart to ours. Jesus said, "Come unto me all ye that labor and are heavy laden and I will give you rest. Take my yoke upon you and learn of me; for I am meek and lowly of heart and ye shall find rest unto your souls. For my yoke is easy and my burden light." (MT 11:28-30). God wants us to keep learning of Him – to know Him better and better.

Getting on the right track is just the beginning. Now we need to learn how to run. Just like great runners and athletes in all sports, the Christian needs to train and discipline himself to win the Prize (i.e. Christ). The Prize will be discussed further in the next chapter.

When we come to Christ, our old paradigm of values and behaviors comes with us. Over time, these values and behaviors are transformed into a new Christ-centered paradigm - with Christ's values and behaviors. This transformation and learning process, however, requires discipline. Unlike regular athletes who prepare **before** the race, the Christian race itself provides the training opportunities. In fact, disciplining ourselves is an essential element of running the race God's way. The discipline is required to keep us fit and strong. It allows the Holy Spirit to shape us into Christ's image (RO 12:1-2). This happens as we discipline ourselves to regularly study the Word, Pray, Worship, Fellowship, and Serve. If just a fraction of the time we waste would be used to study the Word, pray, witness to others, visit and fellowship with a friend in need, or comfort someone who is hurting, what a difference it would make for both the visible and invisible kingdom of God. EPH 5: 16 encourages us to be wise and redeem the time.

To make our discipline perfect, our Lord also allows us to go through Trials and Suffering. The Christian life is not an easy life - but it **is** the abundant life.

Training and discipline in a Christian's life is extremely important. We need to be competent and confident in the things of our Lord. We honor the name of our Master Teacher when we are faithful to learn from Him – when we maintain a "teach me" attitude – when we make knowing Him the highest goal of our learning. However, it is also true that God uses all Christians, where they are now, who surrender to Him for service, as He shapes us into what He wants us to become. A little becomes a lot in God's hands. God seems to specialize in using a weak instrumentality to get great results:

- Moses' rod (EX 4:2) – Among other miracles, God told Moses to lift up his rod and stretch it out over the Red Sea and divide it so Israel could escape the Egyptians and go across on dry ground.
- The jawbone of a mule (JU 15:15) – Samson killed 1000 Philistines with it.
- Five smooth stones (1 SA 17:40,49) – David killed Goliath with one smooth stone .
- A handful of meal and a little oil (1 KI 17:12,16) – It sustained the widow of Zarephath, her son, and Elijah during a three year drought.
- A cloud the size of a man's hand (1 KI 18:44-45) – God caused a great rain after a three year drought.

The training and discipline in a Christian's life – the process of learning to run the race well - can be compared to riding a bicycle:

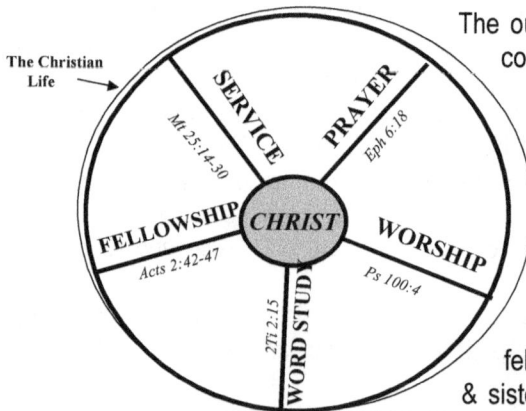

The outside rim of the wheel is connected to the hub by means of spokes. The rim is our Christian Life. The hub is Christ. We need to keep our life connected to Christ by 5 very important spokes - prayer, study of the Word, worship, fellowship with our brothers & sisters in Christ, and serving God by using the talents that God has given every Christian.

The sixth spoke consists of the trials our Lord allows us to endure. There are struggles for us all – but sometimes we cause our own problems and make the ride "bumpy" for several reasons:

- Christ must be in the center of our lives – the "hub" of the wheel. We often put ourselves back in that place.
- The spokes need to be kept in balance – some of us love to worship regularly - but only study the Word when necessary. Some love to study but sharing their life in fellowship is too "close". Different size spokes cause a rough ride.
- As the spokes get longer, pumping the bike to go forward farther is easier because the wheel is bigger. If the spokes are short, however, we have to pump hard to cover just a short distance because the wheel is small.

As we run for our lives God's way, we need to make the course of our lives a journey that we savor. Knowing God and being like Christ is our goal. Prayer, Word Study, Worship, Fellowship, Service, and Trials/Suffering are the highways where we will find our Divine Running Partner and Coach, Jesus Christ. They are the pathways He has carved with His own footprints, the exercise gear to strengthen and shape us, the guideposts to mark off the course, and the track shoes to securely grip the grains of shifting sand on the race track of our lives. "My soul longeth, yea, even fainteth for the courts of the Lord: my heart and my flesh crieth out for the living God...Blessed is the man whose strength is in thee; in whose heart are *the highways to Zion*." (R.V.) (PS 84:2,5)

Pray for knowing God's purposes (JA 1:5) – for the servant leader mind and heart of Christ to disciple others – for the needs of others with whom we fellowship: things they share with us and also things we desire for them because we love them and are concerned (EPH 6:18). How should we pray? Meet the Lord in prayer everyday at the same time. Make it your appointment with Him. Pray in your own words and use the guideline that Jesus gave us in LK 11:1-4 and MT 6: 9-13:

- "Hallowed be Thy name" – Worship the Lord with praise – a bouquet of words that proclaim who He is: Our Father, the blessed controller of all things. No matter what is happening, He will work all things together for good to those who love Him and are called according to His purpose (RO 8:28). Tell Him that the kingdom, the power, and the glory are His.
- "Our Father" – Let Him know in your own words that He owns you and that everything you are and have are His. You hold yourself and what

you have out to Him with an "open hand" not "closed fisted" so whatever He wants to use, He may do so with your approval. Ask Him to "give us this day our daily bread" – that He meet all your daily needs. Since He is Father of your brothers and sisters in Christ (i.e. "Our Father"), ask for the needs of others too.

- "Thy kingdom come, Thy will be done on earth as it is in heaven" – Seek to understand His kingdom (i.e. the invisible, the visible, and the kingdom of heaven). Then pray for the earth to be recovered for Him – Pray for His strength to take your stand for Christ in the territory of your home, school, workplace, church, etc.) – Pray for the return of Christ to deliver the kingdoms of this world to our heavenly Father (REV 11:15).

- "Forgive us our sins as we forgive everyone indebted to us" – Pray that God would soften your heart towards others according to His will – that you'd be "tender-hearted forgiving others as God, for Christ's sake has forgiven you" (EPH 4:32).

- "Lead us not into temptation, but deliver us from evil." – Pray for His help in "keeping God's armor on" – to understand the spiritual authority of Christ's ambassador and friend – to help you and your brothers and sisters in Christ to take their stand – to hold their position for Christ (EPH 6: 10-18),

Study the Word to know Christ – to wear well the "blood-covering" and "the armor of God" – to find out how the race course is marked (i.e. its limits, boundaries, valleys and mountaintops) – to be sure we're on the right track – to develop a genuine love for others on the team running with us (EPH 2:6, 19-22) – to allow the Holy Spirit to empower us to run well.

The Gideons, International have said, " The Bible contains the mind of God, the state of man, the way of salvation, the doom of sinners, and the happiness of believers. It's doctrines are holy, its precepts are binding, its histories are true, and its decisions are immutable. Read it to be wise, believe it to be safe, and practice it to be holy. It contains light to direct you, food to support you, and comfort to cheer you.

It is the traveler's map, the pilgrim's staff, the pilot's compass, the soldier's sword, and the Christian's charter. Here Paradise is restored, heaven opened, and the gates of hell disclosed. Christ is its grand subject, our good the design, and the glory of God its end.

It should fill the memory, rule the heart, and guide the feet. Read it slowly, frequently, and prayerfully. It is a mine of wealth, a paradise of glory, and a river of pleasure. It is given you in life, will be opened at the judgment, and be remembered forever. It involves the highest responsibility, will reward the greatest labor, and will condemn all who trifle with its sacred contents."

Surrender for service to allow Him to use us for His glory and for honoring His name – to let Him bless us as a vessel He works through as fathers and husbands, mothers and wives, church leaders, workplace leaders, and believers fulfilling the Great Commission – to develop a heart in us for serving others (LK 12:35) – to develop hearts in others we disciple for serving like He's developed in us.

Jesus told His disciples, "Launch out into the deep, and let down your nets for a draught." (LK 5:4). Though they had fished all night and caught nothing, they obeyed the Master. They caught so many fish that their net was breaking and they had to call "their partners" to help them. As they did, let us be obedient to the Lord and overcome our fear to get into deep waters with Him where the "fishing for souls" and making disciples is good. It's in deep water where we must depend upon His strength and not our own. Let's surrender for service as He calls us, overcome our fears, and trust Him to do the work through us by His Holy Spirit.

Worship to tell Him how much we love Him and how much we appreciate His work in our lives – to realize and enjoy being in His presence – to remind ourselves who He is and who we are in Christ. Worship Him as the Lord and the One we serve. Enjoy His great love and acceptance of us as He shapes us into what He wants us to be. PS 95: 1-6 gives us guidelines in worshipping our great God:

"O come, let us sing unto the Lord: let us make a joyful noise to the rock of our salvation. Let us come before his presence with thanksgiving, and make a joyful noise unto him with psalms. For the Lord is a great God, and a great King above all gods. In his hands are the deep places of the earth: the strength of the hills is his also. The sea is his, and he made it: and his hands formed the dry land. O come, let us worship and bow down: let us kneel before the Lord our maker."

As we worship Him as our Lord, let's remember to be liberal in our giving to His work – our time, money, talents, and strength. "But this I say, He which soweth sparingly shall reap also sparingly; and he which soweth bountifully shall also reap bountifully. Every man according as he purposeth in his heart, so let him give; not grudgingly, or of necessity: for God loveth a cheerful giver." (2COR 9:6-7).

Fellowship with brothers and sisters in Christ. We do this by submitting to each other (EPH 5:21), being accountable to one another, and sharing

remember...

*We don't appreciate **fellowship** until our natural man is dealt with through the disciplinary work of the Holy Spirit. When Jacob reached Hebron (Gen 35:27), he was ready for fellowship.*

When we reach Hebron, we are ready to receive Christ from others. That's what fellowship is all about...

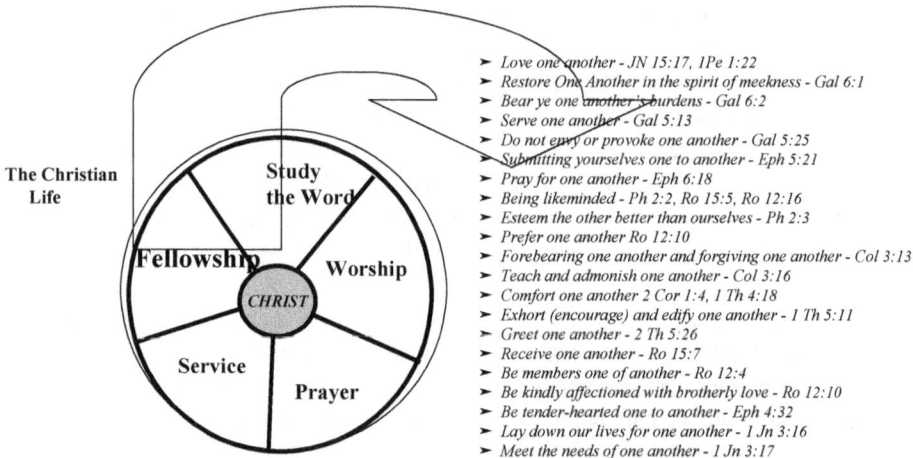

The Christian Life

Study the Word

Fellowship

Worship

CHRIST

Service

Prayer

➤ *Love one another - JN 15:17, 1Pe 1:22*
➤ *Restore One Another in the spirit of meekness - Gal 6:1*
➤ *Bear ye one another's burdens - Gal 6:2*
➤ *Serve one another - Gal 5:13*
➤ *Do not envy or provoke one another - Gal 5:25*
➤ *Submitting yourselves one to another - Eph 5:21*
➤ *Pray for one another - Eph 6:18*
➤ *Being likeminded - Ph 2:2, Ro 15:5, Ro 12:16*
➤ *Esteem the other better than ourselves - Ph 2:3*
➤ *Prefer one another Ro 12:10*
➤ *Forebearing one another and forgiving one another - Col 3:13*
➤ *Teach and admonish one another - Col 3:16*
➤ *Comfort one another 2 Cor 1:4, 1 Th 4:18*
➤ *Exhort (encourage) and edify one another - 1 Th 5:11*
➤ *Greet one another - 2 Th 5:26*
➤ *Receive one another - Ro 15:7*
➤ *Be members one of another - Ro 12:4*
➤ *Be kindly affectioned with brotherly love - Ro 12:10*
➤ *Be tender-hearted one to another - Eph 4:32*
➤ *Lay down our lives for one another - 1 Jn 3:16*
➤ *Meet the needs of one another - 1 Jn 3:17*

life – our testimony, our victories and struggles, our appointments and disappointments ---our relationship with Jesus Christ. We fellowship when we share how our Lord is both our possessor and dis-possessor as we surrender our life to Him. We fellowship when we receive Christ from one another by obeying His "one another" instructions.

Trials/suffering – There is no trial or temptation we undergo that isn't common to other men and women. God is always faithful and will not allow us to be tempted above what we are able to bear. He will always provide a way to escape so that we'll be able to bear it. (1 COR 10:13). The Apostle Peter said that the trial of our faith through the pressures of life is much more precious than of gold that is tried in the fire (1PE 1:7). Just like the goldsmith knows when he sees his image in the gold that it is purified and ready, our Father wants to see His Son's image in us. He is careful to make the fire hot enough but not too hot to break the vessel. 1 PE 4:12-13 says, "Beloved, think it not strange concerning the fiery trial which is to try you, as though some strange thing happened unto you: But rejoice, in as much as ye are partakers of Christ's sufferings; that when his glory shall be revealed, ye may be glad also with exceeding joy." As a fine jeweler, He is "cutting" the stones perfectly to create the precious jewels that are the foundation of His "showcase city" – the New Jerusalem (REV 21:19-20).

Esther Kerr Rusthoi reminds us in her song "When We See Jesus" that all the trials and suffering will be worth it all: "It will be worth it all when we see Jesus. Life's trials will seem so small when we see Christ; One glimpse at His dear face, all sorrow will erase, So bravely run the race till we see Christ."

He never leaves us alone during our trials. He is an ever-present comfort through them all. 2COR 1: 3 - 5 explains what God does in us with the trials and suffering we experience. "Praise be to the God and Father of our Lord Jesus Christ, the Father of compassion and the God of all comfort, who comforts us in all our troubles, so we can comfort those in any trouble with the comfort we ourselves have received from God."

When you pour water into a glass, the glass overflows with water. But when suffering is poured into the Christian's life, over time the Holy Spirit performs a miracle in our lives. Instead of the bitterness, anger, and self-pity that suffering could cause pouring out of the Christian, the comfort of God that comforted us during our trials overflows from us to others who are hurting. That may take the form of comforting words, a hug, a kiss, and sometimes just helping them cry. Jesus showed us (e.g. with Mary and Martha when Lazarus died) that He wants us to share in another's sorrow. It's our very personal relationship to our heavenly Father through Jesus Christ that gets us through trials and helps us allow the Holy Spirit to use them to benefit us and others. As we run the Christian race, we can become at times so hunkered down by our problems that we lose proper perspective. Our

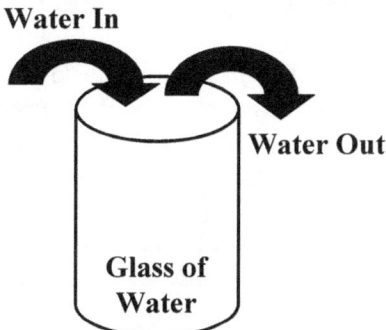

problems look big and the power of God looks small. At those times, we need to draw close to our Father and let Him minister to us as He does in IS 40:15, 22. God reminds us in these scriptures that He is much bigger than the world He created.

The eagle, when it senses a storm approaching, flies to the highest peak it can find and waits. When the storm arrives, it extends its wings and lets the wind take it safely above the storm. Similarly, God ministers to us, directs our actions, and gets us through the storms of life. He says, "But they that wait upon the

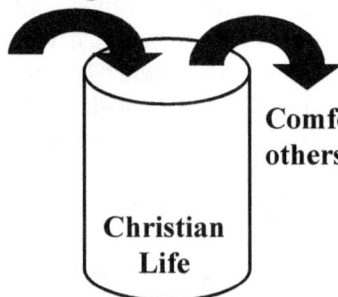

Suffering In

Comfort to others Out

Christian Life

Lord shall renew their strength; they shall mount up with wings as eagles; they shall run, and not be weary; and they shall walk and not faint." (IS 40:31)

Remember the three Hebrews who were thrown into the fire for not worshipping the image of gold made by Nebuchadnezzar. The Babylonian king said, "I see four men loose, walking in the midst of the fire, and they have no hurt; and the form of the fourth is like the Son of God." (DAN 3:25) We're never in the fire alone. RO8: 28 tells us , "All things work together for good to those that love God and are called according to His purposes."

Our divine "Coach" uses all six of these training opportunities (i.e. Word study, prayer, worship, fellowship, service, and trials/suffering) and our life's experiences "on the track" to transform us into Christ's image (EPH 4:13). As we discipline ourselves in each of these areas of the Christian life, the Holy Spirit is faithful to transform us. As we are being transformed, we're always about our Father's business of making disciples – obeying the Great Commission (MT 28:19) - cooperating with the Holy Spirit to evangelize the lost and help shape our brothers and sisters into the Christlike servant-leaders our Father wants us all to be.

As Great Commission disciple-makers, we need to embrace the values and behaviors that make Christ great. Stay fit. Spiritually over weight and flabby runners cannot fulfill their responsibilities to our "Coach" and our teammates.

Chapter 5

Run For The Prize
The New Paradigm Values

Liv always had a problem with loneliness. The worst thing about his tour in Vietnam was being away from his wife and kids. One day, after he had been a Christian a short time, his wife and kids left for a three week vacation back home. Liv was left alone. So he filled his days with the Lord – truly Jesus became everything to him. Every spare moment outside of the work site was used to listen to Christian music (with earphones on), to read the Word of God, or to pray. One day Liv was lying on his bed, with his hands outstretched and eyes opened, praying to our Lord. In those days, he always tried to impress God with his prayers – make them sound very flowery, using a lot of "thee" and "thou" and creating word pictures using streams, birds, mountains, and valleys. Now there would have been nothing wrong with that except that Liv's motives weren't pure – he wanted to impress God.

As he prayed, Liv began to see a small white cloud forming in the hallway just outside his bedroom. The cloud was moving slowly towards him. As it moved to a position just over him, Liv's heart was pounding wildly and his prayers were becoming much shorter and louder. As the cloud began moving downward upon him, Liv closed his eyes and began shouting short prayers – like "Save my Dad and Mom!" – "Save my family!" – "Use me Lord!" He didn't know how long that lasted, but after a while, his heart became normal again and he opened his eyes. The cloud was gone and so was any attempt to impress the Lord. Liv found out later that this was a "visitation" from God for His own reasons. His life after that experience began to be more honest and open in his relationship with God and others. Holiness meant so much more now.

During the same three-week period, Liv went to visit some friends who lived about 40 miles away. On the way back, he was singing to the Lord while speeding down the highway. Five small clouds in the sky caught his eye. "How strange having five small clouds in a row like that", he thought. As he kept singing, and running his eyes back and forth between those clouds, Liv realized that the clouds were actually letters standing next to each other. They spelled as clear as if they were written on a blackboard: J E S U S. At first he looked to see if any other cars were stopping to stare at the clouds, then he just sang even louder with more joy in his heart as he proceeded home. Liv realized how intimate Jesus really wanted to be with him – this was a real personal relationship with a Lord who wants to touch our hearts in whatever way He can.

The church that Liv was attending encouraged reading the entire Word of God through each year. The pastor would review the reading on Wednesday nights. Because his family was away, Liv decided to read that week's passage on the church grounds – in the picnic grove. The sun was setting and it caught Liv's eye as it twinkled and glistened between the branches of the trees. As he kept staring at it, Liv began to see what looked like a big eye staring back at him. After a while, he realized it happened as a result of the sun's reflection on his glasses. As he turned to the scripture, he read, "Arise shine for thy light is come, and the glory of the Lord is risen upon thee. For, behold, the darkness shall cover the earth, and gross darkness the people: but the Lord shall arise upon thee, and his glory shall be seen upon thee." (IS 60:1-2) The image of a huge eye and that scripture meant a lot to Liv. He realized the importance of keeping his eyes on the Lord because that's how we see ourselves best. He's like a mirror that reflects how we really look. And as we keep our eyes upon Christ and follow Him, that reflection will look more and more like Christ Himself – the glory will fall on us for others to see!

As we run the race, we need to be transformed to have a Christ-centered world view, as well as Christ's values and behaviors. We need a new paradigm for living. HE 12:1 advises us to "...lay aside the weight and the sin that so easily besets, and run with patience the race that is set before us, looking unto Jesus, the Author and Finisher of our faith..." We need to keep our eyes stayed upon Christ as we patiently and courageously run.

Run For the Prize – Biblical Principles and Application

As we draw near to God (JA 4:8), we put to death our critical, rebellious, selfish, and sinful ways (COL 3:5). The old patterns (i.e. old paradigm) of living cannot survive. The closer we get in our relationship with the Lord the more we leave the world behind. COL 3:1 encourages us to seek those things that are above, where Christ is seated at the right hand of God.

The events in the lives of Elijah and Elisha help us to understand what this means and how we are to run for our lives God's way. God was about to take Elijah home and so Elisha asked Elijah for a double portion of his spirit. Elijah told him that in order to have that double portion, the prophet would have to see God take him home. If he did, then Elijah would drop his mantle for Elisha and he would in deed have a double portion of his spirit.

This idea of "watching" is very important to "winning" the Christian race. "Watching" Jesus helps us win "The Prize" of the race. That Prize is Christ – shaped into His image. As we watch and follow Him we will become more like Him. In PH 3: 13, the Apostle Paul says, "Not as though I have already attained, but this one thing I do: Forgetting what is past and reaching forth to what is before, I press toward the mark toward the prize of the high calling of God in Christ Jesus." In PH 3: 8, 14, and 10 he tells us what the prize is: "...and I count all things but loss for the excellency of the knowledge of Christ Jesus my Lord: for whom I have suffered the loss of all things, and do count them but dung (i.e. trash), that I may win Christ." "I press toward the mark for the prize of the high calling of God in Christ Jesus." "To know Him – the fellowship of His sufferings and the power of His resurrection" (i.e. to know Him and be like Him).

Many of us are familiar with Psalm 23: "The Lord is my shepherd, I shall not want. He maketh me to lie down in green pastures: he leadeth me beside the still waters..." Do you know that Jesus Christ, Himself, is the "green pastures" and "still waters"? He is the nourishment that energizes us to run for our life God's way. Jesus said of Himself, "I am the bread of life: he that cometh to me shall never hunger; and he that believeth on me shall never thirst." (JN 6:35). If we do not allow Jesus to satisfy our hunger and thirst, we will starve. There's a thirst that only He can quench. It's like the marathon runners who must consume water to keep pressing ahead. These runners reach out to grab a bottle of water from a stranger along the course because they know it's critical to winning. "Like the hart (i.e. deer) panteth after the water brooks, so panteth my soul after thee, O God." (PS 42:1). Sheep are afraid of a moving stream – running water – so the Lord leads us to "still waters" (i.e. Himself) where His perfect love casts out our fear and we drink freely and abundantly from Him drawing strength to continue running. Often as we run, the Lord beckons us to Himself – to rest a while in green pastures at the still waters – to regain our strength.

Jesus is also "The Finish Line" of our race – to be like Him. Runners "kick" hardest when they are in the final turn and "see" the finish line just ahead! To help us "see" Christ, the Scripture is replete with "portraits of Christ". Three are presented below - Paul's, Isaiah's, and John's portraits. I believe that the Gospel of John presents the best portrait because each chapter portrays a different aspect of His character. Let the following illustrations help you "see" Christ as you study these books:

Paul's Pictures of Christ

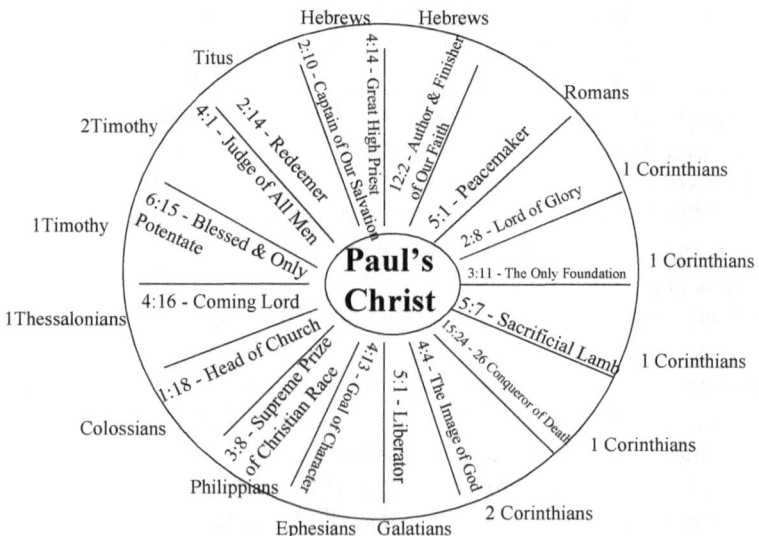

Book of Isaiah - Portrait of Christ

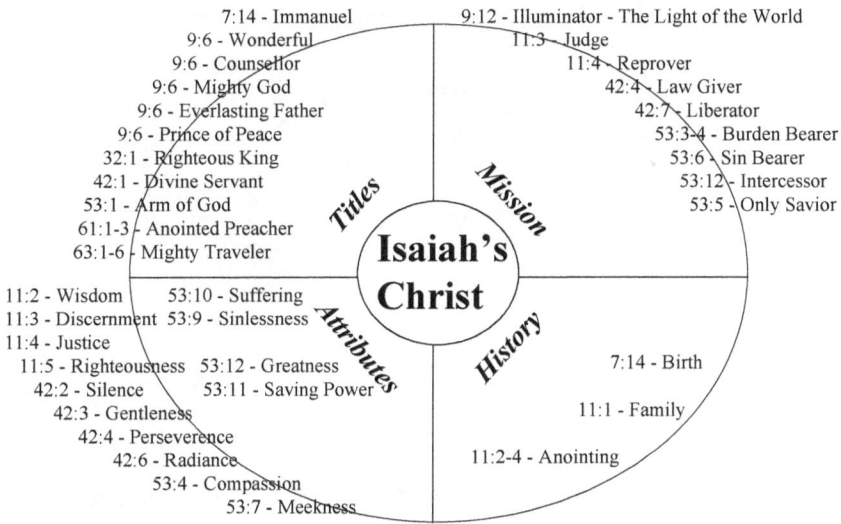

```
        7:14 - Immanuel              9:12 - Illuminator - The Light of the World
      9:6 - Wonderful                   11:3 - Judge
      9:6 - Counsellor                     11:4 - Reprover
      9:6 - Mighty God                      42:4 - Law Giver
     9:6 - Everlasting Father               42:7 - Liberator
     9:6 - Prince of Peace                    53:3-4 - Burden Bearer
    32:1 - Righteous King                      53:6 - Sin Bearer
    42:1 - Divine Servant                      53:12 - Intercessor
    53:1 - Arm of God                          53:5 - Only Savior
   61:1-3 - Anointed Preacher
   63:1-6 - Mighty Traveler
                            Titles   Mission
                              Isaiah's
 11:2 - Wisdom    53:10 - Suffering
 11:3 - Discernment 53:9 - Sinlessness  Christ
 11:4 - Justice                    Attributes  History
  11:5 - Righteousness 53:12 - Greatness
   42:2 - Silence       53:11 - Saving Power      7:14 - Birth
    42:3 - Gentleness
     42:4 - Perseverance                    11:1 - Family
      42:6 - Radiance
       53:4 - Compassion        11:2-4 - Anointing
        53:7 - Meekness
```

Elisha followed Elijah wherever he went and never let him out of his sight. When God sent the fiery chariot to speed Elijah home, Elisha was faithfully watching his master and Elijah dropped his mantle for him. Immediately, Elisha went to see if he had a double portion of Elijah's spirit. He picked up the mantle and went to the Jordan river. He cracked the mantle on the river and said, "Where is the God of Elijah?" The Jordan parted and he walked across on dry ground. He had that double portion of God's spirit and from then on did many exploits for God.

As Elisha followed Elijah and saw God take him home, and received the double portion of Elijah's spirit, let us "follow" our Lord in His values and behaviors. Let us take up the mantle of the Holy Spirit which Christ has "dropped" to help us make disciples of all nations. Let us follow Him closely and emulate what we see in Him.

remember...

The Gospel of John

Gives Sight To The Blind

Chp 1 - The Son of God
Chp 2 - The Son of Man
Chp 3 - The Divine Teacher
Chp 4 - The Soul Winner
Chp 5 - The Great Physician
Chp 6 - The Bread of Life
Chp 7 - The Water of Life
Chp 8 - The Defender of the weak
Chp 9 - The Light of the World
Chp 10 - The Good Shepherd

Chp 11 - The Prince of Life
Chp 12 - The King   13 - The Servant
Chp 14 - The Consoler
Chp 15 - The True Vine
Chp 16 - The Giver of the Holy Spirit
Chp 17 - The Great Intercessor
Chp 18 - The Model Sufferer
Chp 19 - The Uplifted Savior
Chp 20 - The Conqueror of Death
Chp 21 - The Restorer of
the Penitent

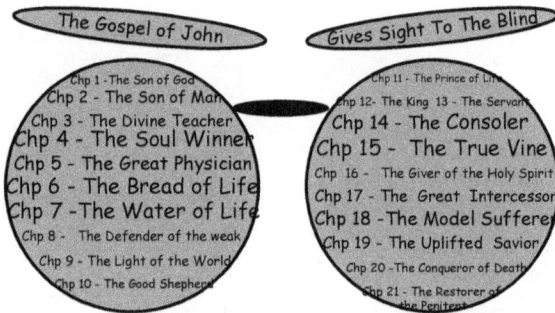

The Gospel of John is specially designed to help us get to know our Lord Jesus Christ better. Each Chapter presents Him in a unique aspect of who He is. Lenny received Jesus as his Lord and Savior after reading John 10 about how He is The Good Shepherd and knows His sheep and is known by them - that made him see how the Lord wanted a personal relationship with him.

When someone is seeking to know more about the Christian Life, let them read this Gospel first - it will help them see Christ more clearly and completely.

Every Christian is a leader. We exercise influence over people in our various roles. We are husbands and wives who influence our spouses. We are fathers and mothers who influence our children. We are workplace supervisors who influence our employees. We are coaches who lead sports teams. We are church leaders – teachers, deacons, pastors, elders, trustees, ministry leaders, etc. – who influence our brothers and sisters in Christ. We may "touch" people in hospitals, nursing homes, soup kitchens, rescue missions, or as we visit the sick, feed the hungry, cloth the naked, visit the prisoners, and give water to the thirsty. As Great Commission believers – lieutenants in Christ's army – ambassadors of Christ – we influence men, women, and children to come to Christ and we help them grow spiritually mature. We influence those with whom we fellowship wherever God has set us in the church.

As leaders who exercise influence, we need to become "the roar of the crowd" in other people's lives. Our values and behaviors as individuals in God's kingdom within us and as the church of the visible kingdom should overcome the influence of the world, flesh, and the devil. "Be of good cheer, I have overcome the world." (JN 16:33) "...I will build my church:

and the gates of hell shall not prevail against it." (MT 16:18) "Be not overcome of evil, but overcome evil with good." (RO 12:21)

Every Christian is a leader. We need to keep our eyes on the Leader of leaders, King of kings, Lord of lords, who is always the Lamb upon the throne – the Servant of servants. As we run for our lives God's way, we need to "see" Jesus, who ran the race before us to show us how to run well. *What did He leave us as a legacy of values and behaviors to emulate as we run the Christian race? How can we be the ambassadors of His grace and influence lives like He does? How do we live and lead in His likeness?*

Trying to describe Jesus' values and behaviors in a few words is impossible – it's like an ordinary person trying to describe a star or a collection of stars. All we can do is really point someone in the right direction and let them take in all the beauty their eyes can see there. That's what we'll try to do in this chapter. Our precious Lord has given me Elijah's mantle as a way to help us "see" this Christlike paradigm for living. You can study further by reading one of my other books entitled *The Mantle: How To Dress For Success In Leadership.*

There was a professor who brought a wide mouth jar into his classroom one day. He set it in front of his class and began filling it with large rocks. When the rocks were up to the rim of the jar, he asked his class, "Is the jar filled?" They said, "It sure is." So the professor proceeded to pour gravel into the cracks between the stones. Again he asked if the jar was filled. But this time the class knew this clever professor wasn't finished. He then took some sand and filled the cracks between all the gravel until the jar was packed solid. "Is it filled now?", he asked. Everyone thought it was until he took out a jar of water and poured it into the sand. He then told his class that the jar represented their lives and asked them what lesson they had learned from this demonstration. One smart young student replied that it meant that you could always fit more into a busy life! The professor, however, was not teaching that lesson. He said, "The lesson is that you better get the big rocks into your life before you start adding other things." As Christians, we need to get the foundational Christ-values into our lives – the important things – before we start adding all the activities that make up that life. So here are the foundational values (i.e. big rocks)...

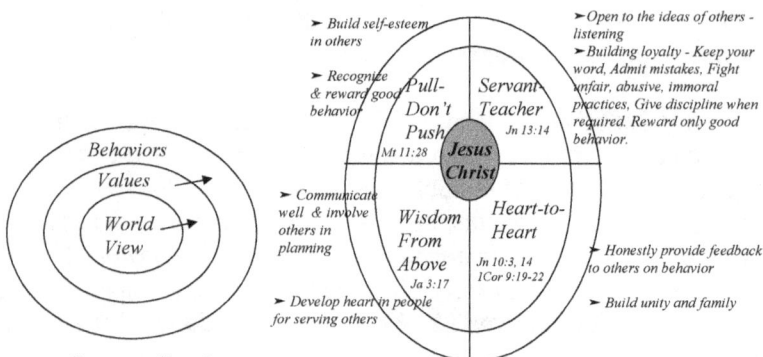

Before coming to Christ, our world view has US in the center. This shapes our values and our behaviors. This creates a paradigm for living - all the rules for life and how we measure success.

When we come to Christ, our old paradigm of values and behaviors comes with us. Over time, these values and behaviors are changed into the Christ-centered paradigm above- 4 values and 8 behaviors. We are transformed (Ro12:1-2) by studying the Word, Prayer, Worship, Fellowship, Service, and Trials/Suffering.

Growth is faster both for us and others if we obey the Great Commission (Mt 28:19) and "teach all nations.." - those that God has set us with in the local body. As Great Commission disciple-makers, we need to embrace the values and behaviors that make Christ great - the four values are found in the cross: ST (Jn 3:16); HTH (Ro 5:8); WFA (2Cor 5:21); PDP (Ph 2:7-8; Mt 16:24)

Servant Leader/Teacher. The first value is called Servant – Teacher or Servant –Leader. Elijah's mantle may have been a pillow, blanket, ground covering, or shelter for him. It served him. We Christians need to value serving others. All Christians find themselves to be leader/teachers - we may be fathers or mothers, husbands or wives, secular teachers or workplace supervisors/team leaders, deacons or other church leaders, and also Great Commission teachers making disciples in accordance with MT 28:19. " Go and teach all nations…"

Jesus said, " He who is greatest among you will be your servant." (MT 23:11). At another occasion, before His crucifixion, Jesus laid aside His garments, wrapped a towel around Himself, and began washing the disciples feet and wiping them with the towel. When He finished, He said to them, " You call me Teacher and Lord, and you say well for so I am. If I, then, your Lord and Teacher have washed your feet, you also ought to wash one another's feet. For I have given you an example that you should do as I have done…If you know these things, happy are you if you do them." (JN 13:13-17). Jesus also said, at another time, "Whoever desires to be first among you, let him be your slave – just as the Son of Man did not come to be served, but to serve, and to give His life a ransom for many." (MT 20:27-28).

These remarks by our Lord Jesus Christ, who is King of kings and Lord of lords, but also forever the Lamb upon the throne, speak volumes about the importance He places upon *serving*. As "Christ" (i.e. Anointed One), Jesus is now (and was on the cross) our intercessor between God and man. As Old Testament priests served the people by offering up sacrifices for their sins and getting the people in communion with God, Christ offered Himself up as an atoning sacrifice for the sins of the world. So then, as commissioned leaders making disciples, we must value serving others if we are going to emulate Christ as we run the Christian race.

Heart-To-Heart. The second value is called heart-to-heart. It's placing importance upon getting to know the people we are leading or teaching and letting them get to know us as well. Elijah's mantle "knew" every part of his body – it hugged him. As he wore it, the mantle felt his heartbeat. We need to "feel the heartbeat" of our people. Many Christians forget the whole reason Jesus came to earth. It wasn't just to save us. Thank God that He did that for us – The relationship with our heavenly Father was broken and His heart was broken as well. Jesus came to restore that relationship by paying the price for our sin – death.

He also came, however, so we could get our arms around God – to "hug Him". The world had lost its knowledge of God – then, like now, there were many ideas about what God was like. Jesus said, " He who has seen me, has seen the Father." (JN 14:9). The Apostle John also said about getting to know God, "In the beginning was the Word and the Word was with God...and the Word was God...and the Word became flesh and dwelt among us." JN 1: 1- 14. In his first letter, John says, "That which was from the beginning, which we have heard, which we have seen with our eyes, which we have looked upon, and our hands have handled, of the Word of life..." (1 JN 1:1)

As far as getting to know us, Jesus said, "I am the good shepherd, and I know My sheep and am known by My own." (JN 10:14). Speaking of the good shepherd, Jesus said, " To him the doorkeeper opens; and the sheep hear his voice; and he calls his own sheep by name and he leads them out." (JN 10:3). Jesus knows what it's like to be you and me. He cares about our every concern. He even cares enough to have every hair on each of our heads numbered. (MT 10:30)

Jesus always valued taking the time to get to know people and to meet their needs. Remember blind Bartemaeus. Jesus was headed for Jerusalem, and when Bartemaeus heard that it was Jesus of Nazereth who was passing by, he called out to Him, "Jesus, thou son of David, have mercy on me." (LK18: 38). His disciples told the old man to keep still and not bother the Master. But Jesus wanted to know this man's heart. He said, " What wilt thou that I do unto thee?" Zacchaeus was another who wanted to get to know Jesus – and he wasn't disappointed. Jesus looked up into the tree, where this corrupt tax collector had positioned himself to catch a glimpse of the Master, and said, "Zacchaeus, make haste, and come down; for today I must abide at your house." (LK19: 5)

We too need to value being heart-to-heart with the people our Lord has given to us.

Wisdom From Above. James 3:17 says that, "The wisdom that is from above is first pure, then peaceable, gentle, willing to yield, full of mercy and good fruits (some translations say goodness, fairness, genuineness), without partiality, and without hypocrisy." Like Jesus, we need to value these qualities – primarily being *pure*. We need to have pure motives and be a person that can be trusted by others to help them through the "storms" of their lives. Many surveys of employees have been done to determine what kind of supervisor they want. The most important quality they want is *integrity – someone they can trust.*

Elijah's mantle can help us understand the importance of having pure motives and integrity. The mantle was a sleeveless garment made of the skins of animals with the hair left on it. It needed to be thick enough to resist the wind and sand during the storms in the prophet's life. It also couldn't have any tears or holes in it that would let the rain in. In short, it needed to have *integrity* to protect the prophet from the elements. And if we want to help others through the "storms" of their life – to have them share with us their troubles and seek the insights God gives us – then we must also have pure motives and this wisdom from above.

It's helpful to us Christians, running on the "high calling track" (i.e. PH 3: 14), to examine our hearts – to look for this wisdom which is first pure. The way to do that well is to let our Lord Jesus Christ take us on an incredible journey through our hearts. Consider what our Lord might say as He enters each room there. The following is adapted from **My Heart, Christ's Home**, by Robert Boyd Munger, 1986:

In JN 14:23, Jesus said, "If a man loves me he will keep my words: and my Father will love him, and we will come and make our abode with him." A Christian's heart has many rooms. While Jesus is preparing a place for us in heaven (JN 14:3), we are to prepare a place for Him in our hearts. To determine how we're doing, walk through these rooms with Jesus.

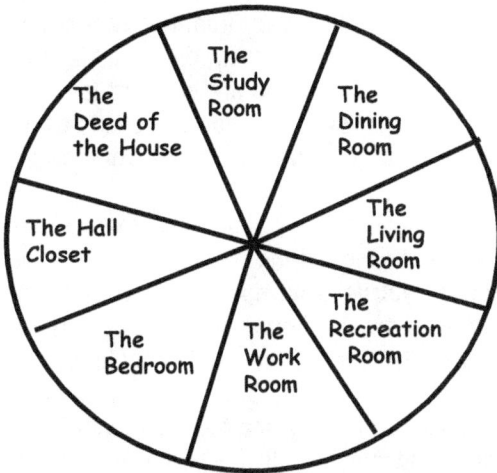

➢ **The Study** – What would Jesus see in your mind? What are the magazines, books, TV programs we read? He would want His picture in the center of that room and the books of the Scriptures on all the book shelves

➢ **The Dining Room** - What would you serve Jesus? What are your appetites and desires? Your education, wealth, investments, awards, etc.? If so, Jesus would not eat much and would say, "I have meat that you know not of – to do the will of my Father who sent me and to finish His work (JN 4:34).

➢ **The Living Room** – This is the room where Jesus waits to meet us everyday. Do you read the Word and pray to Him daily? He would tell you that this time is not just for us but also for Him. He paid a great price for us – and wants to meet and fellowship with us often.

➢ **The Recreation Room** - This is our place of fun and fellowship. Would the Lord find us taking Him with us when we go out with friends – or would we have to tell Him to wait home because He would feel uncomfortable? He would remind us that we were going to let Him be our Friend and go with us everywhere.

➢ **The Work Room** – The Lord would look to see what we've done for Him lately. We might say that we felt awkward and clumsy in spiritual things. He would agree and tell us to put ourselves in the control of the Holy Spirit and let Him lead us in doing God's work.

- ➢ **The Bedroom** – Here the Lord would remind us that He doesn't restrict sex to a marriage relationship because sex is bad but because it is good under the right conditions. When not in marriage, sex can be harmful and destructive.
- ➢ **The Hall Closet** – As we are showing the Lord around our heart, He may pass the hall closet and mention that there's a horrible odor coming from there – maybe some stuff left over from our lives before we asked Him to come in. He'd want us to clean it. We would tell Him that we didn't have the strength – these things are too hard for us to "set aside". But we'd finally ask Him to clean it for us. Jesus would say that He'd been waiting for us to ask. Very soon the closet would be clean.
- ➢ After struggling to keep our hearts *pure,* many of us would then ask the Lord to clean our whole house like He did the hall closet. He would say, "Fine but I can't because you've only made me a guest here. First, you'll need to sign **the deed of your house** over to Me and make Me the owner." So we finally really do make Him Lord of our heart.

So besides valuing serving others and being heart-to heart with them, the Lord wants us to appreciate and embrace this wisdom from above which is first pure.

Pull – Don't – Push. Let's continue using Elijah's mantle to describe this value. A cloth garment has no "push power." When you try to push someone with a mantle, it bends. A cloth garment can't push anything. So as Christian leaders, we shouldn't be twisting our people's arms to make them do something – or backing them into a corner or making them feel guilty or manipulating them into submission. That's not Christ. If we're to emulate Christ, then we need to learn to "wrap our mantle around others" and *draw* them to us – and eventually to Christ.

In MT 7:11, Jesus says, "Come unto me all you are weak and heavy laden, and I will give you rest. Take my yoke upon you and learn about me for I am meek and lowly in heart and will give you rest unto your souls." Jesus draws us to Himself. Even when His requirements seem difficult, we do what He wants us to. For example, "If you want to be my disciple, then deny yourself daily, take up your cross and follow me." If a man loves his family more than me, he is not worthy of me..." We follow Him because He is everything we want to be – and as we follow Him, we are becoming like Him.

These four values can also be seen very vividly in the cross of Christ. The servant-leader value is seen in **the self-sacrifice of the cross** – our Lord's continuing desire to give and to minister rather than be ministered to: " For God so loved the world, that He gave His only begotten Son, that whosoever believes in Him should not perish, but have everlasting life." (John 3:16). The heart-to-heart value may be seen in **the love of the cross** - Christ's knowing us intimately and still being willing to give Himself for us: "But God commendeth His love toward us, in that, while we were yet sinners Christ died for us." (Romans 5:8). The wisdom from above quality which James 3:17 tells us "is first pure" can be seen in **the holiness of the cross** – Christ, being from the beginning without any sin, to take even one sin upon Himself must have been enormously repugnant. He was willing, however, to take not just one sin upon Himself but all the sins of the world: "For He hath made Him to be sin for us, who knew no sin; that we might be made the righteousness of God in Him." (2 Cor 5:21). The pull - don't – push value can be seen in **the humility and obedience of the cross**. Phil 2:5-8 says, "He humbled Himself and became obedient unto death, even the death of the cross." (See also LK 9:23). Jesus saw our debt, which we couldn't pay, and left the beauty of His home and the glory of His position to pay that debt for us. It wasn't the nails that held Jesus to the cross. It was His love for sinners and His passion to please His Heavenly Father – to restore a right relationship between us sinners and His Father.

Do we embrace the things that make Christ great? These Christlike, "cross-stained" values remind us that as Christ-centered commissioned lieutenants, ambassadors, and role-models of Christ, we cannot have the "crown" without the "cross". Our leadership positions in the home, church, workplace, or as believers fulfilling The Great Commission require us to follow Christ in the values that make Him great . We can't take a shortcut to Christlike leadership.

Jesus resisted the temptation to avoid the cross three times: Once at the garden of Gethsemane when He sweat drops of blood (Luke 22:44). Once when Peter told Him that His death wouldn't be necessary and Jesus rebuked him saying, "Get thee behind me Satan..." (Matthew 16:21-23).

Once in the desert - "Again the devil took Him up into an exceeding high mountain, and showed Him all the kingdoms of the world, and the glory of them; And said unto Him, All these things will I give you, if you will fall down and worship me." Jesus refused. (Matthew 4:8-9).

If we want to be effective Christlike leaders, and run for our life God's way, we must embrace the values we find in the Christ of the cross. Let's remember the mantle Christ has passed to us and be sure He finds us properly "dressed and ready for service.." (Luke 12:35) when He comes again.

Chapter 6

Run In His Footprints
The New Paradigm Behaviors

Liv Livright went on to lead many other home Bible studies, his church's involvement in the Billy Graham Crusade, teaching adult Sunday School for 35 years, becoming a Board member and treasurer in churches of various denominations, and substituting for pastors teaching the Word of God at Wednesday church services. He led his church's prayer service and he became an author, convention workshop leader, speaker and trainer in leadership. He also became president of a non-profit Christian Ministries corporation that sponsored a convention every year that drew over 1000 attendees, provided 150 workshops, and over 50 Christian exhibitors.

Liv was active in secular work as well. The federal government, his employer, sent him to MIT for credits toward a PhD in mathematics. Though he spent time working in many places around the world for 14 years, Liv spent most of his career in the computer field at a northern New Jersey Army research and development center. He eventually retired from there as the Chief Information Officer. For nine years, Liv managed the Operations Branch. It consisted of 150 people and 24 subordinate managers in the areas of computer operations, printing and publishing, illustrations, graphics, exhibits, television production, computer security, technical data processing, and the scientific and technical library. When he was first given that job, there was a Center Commander who managed by fear. He was a perfectionist who threatened and micro-managed his workforce. Liv feared that this leadership philosophy would flow down the ranks and eventually poison all his subordinate managers who would in turn discourage, dishearten, and kill all initiative in his workforce.

So he took about three hours to write down what a good leader should be like. Liv didn't realize it, but by this time, the Lord had imprinted His values and behaviors on Liv's heart and mind. What came about as a result of those few hours of writing can only be explained by crediting the results to God. That philosophy – which Liv called MANagement Thru Leadership (MANTLE), was destined to become the whole Center's philosophy of management and a national basis for measuring leaders. It was all based upon Biblical principles.

At first, his subordinate managers resisted – especially when Liv announced that he and they would be accountable to each other and their people by doing reverse appraisals. That's where the employees get a chance to rate their leaders against the 14 points of the MANTLE leadership philosophy. Steadily, however, Liv's group began winning most of the customer satisfaction awards from a new Center Commander. Soon, Liv's supervisor adopted MANTLE as his philosophy and before long the entire Center had adopted both MANTLE and reverse feedback. When one of his subordinate supervisors retired, he told Liv that at first he frankly thought Liv was crazy for instituting MANTLE and reverse appraisals. But when he saw the change in his employees' attitudes in coming to work, the increase in productivity, and the camaraderie between them, he knew it was the right thing to do.

This northern New Jersey research and development center went on to win many quality awards – partially because of its MANTLE philosophy of leadership. In one year it won three awards: The Presidential Award for Quality (PAQ), which is equivalent to the Malcolm Baldrige Award in industry; The Army Communities of Excellence Award (ACOE); and, The Research and Development Center of the Year Award. Later on, this Center won the New Jersey Governor's award for quality and many others. And it continues to reap the benefits of sowing quality into its products, processes, and leadership. These awards helped to prevent the closure of this government facility and to keep its 3500 employees working.

Liv was delighted whenever he was invited to speak at the many human resources and quality conferences for his employer about MANTLE leadership. Many other government organizations used MANTLE as a benchmark for their own leadership. From coast-to-coast, organizations heard about this award winning leadership philosophy that was based upon Christ's values and behaviors. The Harvard University Kennedy School of Government and the Ford Foundation honored Liv by making MANTLE a semi-finalist in their Innovations in American Government Award competition.

Sometime during those nine years, God called Liv to a ministry of itinerant teaching within the kingdom of God. He was on a "campaign" to bring Christlike leadership to his Jerusalem, Judea, Samaria, and the uttermost parts of the earth. He wasn't accepted well by leaders in many churches, but he kept pressing onward – asking Jesus to guide him. He kept his eyes focused upon the One "who for the joy that was set before him endured the cross, despising the shame, and is set down at the right hand of the throne of God." Wherever God opened the doors of opportunity, Liv was there – Sunday School convention speaker, plenary session speaker, couples retreats, mens retreats, Christian education and ministry convention workshop leader, church dinners, lunches, breakfasts, and (what was always dearest to his heart) adult Sunday School classes in church.

God goes to great lengths to show His unconditional love – especially for the poor, widows, and orphans. For nineteen days, Liv was part of a short-term missions team of pastors and lay people who went to the Philippines. There was an orphanage of 30 children in Tabuk, Kalinga Province that needed help to make needed repairs and also 120 pastors and Christian workers who needed some leadership training. It took 18 hours by air and then 12 hours over two mountain ranges by bus to get there. It was in head-hunter country in the northern most region. Water was undrinkable, bathrooms were outhouses, and the air in Manila and the small towns was thick and polluted by the motorcycles, buses, and "jeepny" vans. The team was prepared to suffer whatever deprivations were necessary to bring God's arms to hug them, hands to help them, and words to encourage and teach them. Liv and the others saw God's footprints in the sand leading to these people and were compelled to follow. The Lord was faithful to his servants as they gave themselves to teach the Filipino pastors, encourage the children, paint their bedrooms, put glass and screens on their windows, minister to health needs, erect basketball backstops, and minister in small churches further in the Philippine interior. The team was forged together in the fire of God's love and strength. He moved and accomplished His will in and through Liv and the others as they followed in the Master's footsteps to "be about Father's business".

Run in His Footprints - Biblical Principles and Application

We don't run for our life God's way in order to earn or work our way into heaven. We've already shown that receiving Jesus Christ – His sacrifice on the cross and glorious resurrection from the dead – is the only way to obtain heaven. As we run, however, we keep our eyes on the Author and Finisher (i.e. the Perfector) – the Starter and the End Result - of our faith. We want to emulate the one whom we love with all our heart, soul, and strength. So we ask, "How should we run for Him?" A better question is, "How should we run from His strength and not our own?" "What can I do to cooperate with Christ in recovering the earth – in making disciples?"

We must first emphasize what Jesus said about making our lives productive . He said, "I am the vine, ye are the branches. He that abideth in me, and I in him, the same bringeth forth much fruit: for without me you can do nothing." (JN 15:5) We are first and foremost not running in our own strength – because nothing done in the flesh (i.e. the natural man) can please Him or fulfill His purposes for our lives. So we produce from Him not for Him. Jesus adds later that producing much fruit this way glorifies His Father and distinguishes us as His disciples. (JN 15:8)

As we embrace Christ's values found in the cross, we do then "seek the kingdom of God and his righteousness." (MT 6: 33) We ask, seek, and knock (MT 6:7-8). We ask Him to make us the servant-leader, who is heart-to-heart with others, with wisdom from above, who doesn't push but rather draws people to himself and ultimately to Christ. We seek opportunities to serve Him in our various roles as husbands, wives, mothers, fathers, workplace leaders, teachers, coaches, church leaders, and disciple makers. We find ourselves often in "deep water" where our abilities are not sufficient. With every spiritual muscle pressed to its limits, only our outstretched hand to His somehow gets us through. We are proactive in walking through the doors God opens for us to minister.

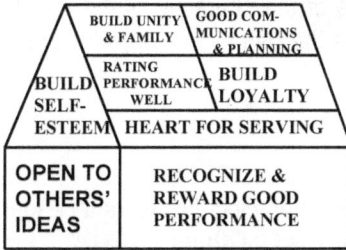

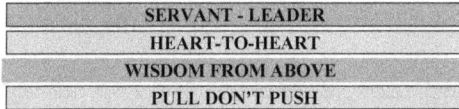

BUILD UNITY & FAMILY	GOOD COM-MUNICATIONS & PLANNING
BUILD SELF-ESTEEM	RATING PERFORMANCE WELL / BUILD LOYALTY
	HEART FOR SERVING
OPEN TO OTHERS' IDEAS	RECOGNIZE & REWARD GOOD PERFORMANCE

SERVANT - LEADER
HEART-TO-HEART
WISDOM FROM ABOVE
PULL DON'T PUSH

As we run with the values of self-sacrifice, love, holiness, humility and obedience, our lives begin to produce much fruit and fragrance. The fruit can be seen, appreciated, and admired, giving glory to our heavenly Father. The fragrance endures. It is transmitted to others who carry it with them as they, in turn, run for their life God's way. The fruit and the fragrance are produced naturally as we allow the Holy Spirit time and as we "wait upon the Lord" (IS 40: 31).

Behaviors Resulting From Embracing Christ's Values

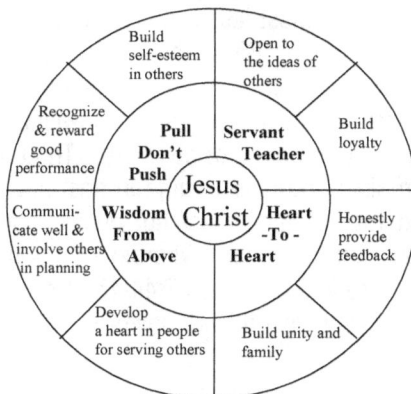

The fruit and fragrance that result from embracing Christ's values are presented as eight distinctive behaviors. These form the visible "house" built solidly upon Christ's foundational values. For each behavior, the prophet's mantle or the character of the prophet himself is briefly mentioned to illustrate the behavior along with examples from Christ's ministry on earth.

SERVANT LEADER/TEACHER

One behavior resulting from embracing the Servant Leader/Teacher value is **Being Open To The Ideas Of Others**

MANTLE GARMENT – It was sleeveless and allowed movement in any direction

This behavior is characterized mostly by listening – not just with our minds but with our hearts. There was a Pharisee named Simon who invited Jesus to his house for a meal. Now in those days, when someone was having guests over, the neighbors were allowed to come in and stand around the wall to observe. As Jesus was reclining at the table, a woman along the wall fell at His feet, began crying and kissing His feet. Her tears fell on His feet as well and she wiped them with her hair. Simon, whose motivation for inviting Jesus was only to find some "flaw" in His character, began thinking that Jesus could not be a prophet if He allowed this harlot to touch Him.

Jesus, however, did not try to avoid the situation. In deed, He heard what the woman was saying to Him and He used the opportunity to teach one of His greatest lessons. He turned to Simon and asked him if he saw this woman. Simon only had a "surface" vision. Jesus looked much deeper. Jesus went on, "I entered into thine house, thou gavest me no water for my feet: but she has washed my feet with tears and wiped them with the hairs of her head. Thou gavest me no kiss: but this woman since the time I came in hast not ceased to kiss my feet. My head with oil thou didst not anoint: but this woman hath anointest my feet with ointment. Wherefore I say unto thee, Her sins, which are many, are forgiven." LK 7:44-47. He went on to show how He felt about forgiving sin - that whoever is forgiven much loves Him the most!

As we run this Christian race, we will come upon those who have been hurt, bruised, beaten down by sin or by life's hardships. In IS 42:3, Isaiah speaks of the coming Messiah as being one who will not "break a bruised reed or quench a smoking flax." Shepherds used to make a flute out of a reed as they tended their sheep. The reed would become too soft and wet in their mouth and they would throw it away. It was good for nothing. That was a "bruised reed". Other shepherds finding that reed would break it because it was worthless in that condition. But Jesus would not break that bruised reed. He would find a way to restore it and make beautiful music from it again. That's what you and I can do by being open to the ideas of people. We need to show – as Jesus would – that they have tremendous value in the hands of the Master. They are creative because they are made in the image of the Creator.

Other examples from Christ's ministry can be found in MK 14: 3-9 and JN 2:1-11.

Another behavior springing from embracing Christ's value of Servant Teacher/Leader is called **Building Loyalty.**

MANTLE GARMENT – The prophet gained confidence in using his mantle. He knew its strengths and versatility in various situations. Those we are discipling need to be confident that our support will always be there for them

Teacher/leaders are the role model for their people. Our relationship to those we influence is reciprocal. Jesus said, "I am the good shepherd: the good shepherd giveth his life for the sheep (JN 10:11). "Servants be obedient to them that are your masters...And, ye masters, do the same things unto them, forebearing threatening: knowing that your Master also is in heaven..." (EPH 6: 5-9). If we want them to listen to us, then we need to listen. If we want respect, then we need to respect. We need to walk our talk and model the behavior we expect from them. For example, we will be the example of prayer – because we are under authority and accountable to God. We will show our people how to pray. That builds loyalty.

We – like Jesus – need to fight unfair systems, immoral and abusive behavior. "It is written, My house is the house of prayer: but ye have made it a den of thieves." (LK 19:46) One day Jesus' disciples were hungry and began to pluck ears of corn and eat it on the sabbath.

When the Pharisees complained, Jesus said, "But if ye had known what this meaneth, I will have mercy, and not sacrifice, ye would not have condemned the guiltless." (MT 12:7)

We need to turn the pyramid upside down in our thinking about leadership. We need to emulate Christ's behavior in washing the disciples' feet (JN 13:13-17) and remember that He said, "But he that is greatest among you shall be your servant." (MT 23:11) We need to serve our people – make them the best disciple they can be so they can then effectively serve others. That also builds loyalty.

"Turning the Pyramid Upside Down"

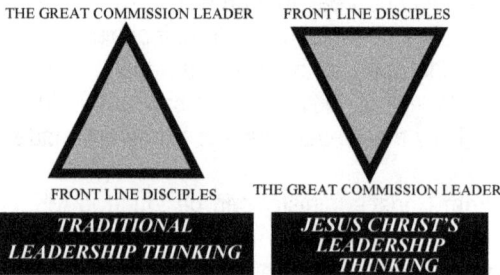

THE GREAT COMMISSION LEADER

FRONT LINE DISCIPLES

FRONT LINE DISCIPLES

THE GREAT COMMISSION LEADER

TRADITIONAL LEADERSHIP THINKING

JESUS CHRIST'S LEADERSHIP THINKING

HEART-TO-HEART

Build Unity And Family is a behavior that flows naturally from valuing being heart-to-heart.

MANTLE GARMENT – It was the badge (i.e. symbol) of the prophet. Elijah and Elisha parted the Jordan with the symbol of the prophet's *office*. This showed that the power rested in the office – not the individual prophet.

If we want to be that ambassador for Christ, we need to emphasize more than just interdependence among the "team" of people God gives us. Knowing that one member depends upon another is important to teach – like Paul did: "For by one spirit are we all baptized into one body, whether we be Jews or Gentiles, whether we be bond or free; and have all been made to drink into one Spirit. For the body is not one member but many. If the foot shall say, Because I am not the hand, I am not of the body; is it therefore not of the body?...And the eye cannot say unto the hand I have no need of thee: not again the head to the feet, I have no need of you…That there should be no schism in the body; but that the members should have the same care one for another." (1COR 12:13-25) In addition to interdependence, we must go further and emphasize family warmth: "But we were gentle among you", Paul said to the Thessalonians, "even as a nurse (i.e. mother) cherisheth her children…" (1TH 2:7). He said that they were as dear to him as a baby would be that is being breast-fed by its mother. As the Lord's lieutenants, we must foster this kind of caring among our people. To tear down barriers between people we can visit them in their homes or when they're sick. We need to bring other "team" members with us.

Remember that Jesus always had time to build caring relationships – no matter how busy He was. He always had time for the Bartimaeus and Zacchaeus. We need to remember that it's a heart commitment we want from people. We want them to truly put their "heart" into what they are doing for us. The connotation in JN 14:15 is, "If you love me, keep my commandments (from the heart)." ACTS 2:42-46 is a description of a "team" that knows they are interdependent and also that they are family. Unity and family were in Jesus' prayer to His Father when He said, "That they all might be one; as thou, Father, art in me, and I in thee, that they also may be one in us…" (JN 17:21)

Another behavior that flows from embracing Christ's heart-to-heart value is to **Honestly Provide Feedback On Performance**

MANTLE GARMENT – The mantle-wearing prophets were used by God to rate how people (often kings) performed. "…thou art weighed in the balances and have been found wanting." (DAN 5:26-28)

As we influence people's lives to receive Christ and then to become mature, we need to set standards for them and ourselves that are truly God's standards. As His prophets spoke the truth (like Daniel above), we also need to speak the truth in love – to give our people honest feedback on performance (EPH 4:15). Encouraging them is always in order. Discouragement is the devil's greatest weapon against Christians. When we must correct them, however, Paul cautions us to do it with meekness. "Brethren, if a man be overtaken in a fault, ye which are spiritual (i.e. mature), restore such an one in the spirit of meekness; considering thyself, lest thou be tempted. Bear ye one another's burdens, and so fulfill the law of Christ." We need to be "meek" in restoring others. Meekness is not weakness. It is the "heart-to-heart' quality in us that responds quickly to the slightest tug by our heavenly Father. It's like a powerful race horse that can be moved with ease by the rider's tug on the reins. We need to listen to God's heart before we correct – but be sure not to avoid correcting.

Get a profile of feedback from other believers for those you disciple. The Lord regularly uses feedback from our brothers and sisters to admonish, encourage, and correct us. Receiving loving, helpful feedback from other Christians, helps us and those we disciple to see our performance from different perspectives. "And I myself am persuaded of you, my brethren, that ye also are full of goodness, filled with all knowledge, able to admonish one another." (RO 15:14) "But exhort one another daily, while it is called today; lest any of you be hardened through the deceitfulness of sin." (HE 3:13) Our feedback to others shouldn't wait for a particular set time. It needs to be "daily". This is especially true when there's a problem. Jesus said, "Therefore if thou bring they gift before the altar, and there rememberest that thy brother has ought against thee; Leave there thy gift before the altar, and go they way; first be reconciled to thy brother, and then come offer thy gift." (MT 5:23-24)

If the Lord gives you a team (i.e. a Bible study group, Sunday School class, discipleship class, home cell group, etc.), you need to provide feedback to them as a team. This is similar to what our Lord did in REV 2 and 3 when He provided feedback to the seven churches. We need to find ways to assess our teams based upon the vision and goals set by the team and also by getting customer (i.e. those served) feedback. Also, as leaders, never be afraid to get feedback on your own performance from the Lord first and also from those you are serving. Remember, even Jesus asked, "Whom do men say that I the Son of man am?" (MT 16:13)

WISDOM FROM ABOVE

As we value the wisdom from above that is first "pure", we will make every effort to provide **Good Communications** and to **Involve Our People In Planning**

MANTLE GARMENT – The mantle was the badge of the prophets, who were God's foremost communicators.

Good Communications. When Jesus is Master of our hearts, our motives will always be pure. We will want to teach our people like parents are instructed to teach their children (PROV 22:6; DEUT 6:7). Communicating to those we are discipling about what affects them is crucial to good performance and satisfaction. Jesus is the Greatest One. MT 5,6, and 7 is the SERMON ON THE MOUNT in which Jesus summarized the essence of life more concisely and with more depth than anyone else has ever done.

On the road to Emmaus, Jesus met two dejected disciples. They were discouraged over the events about Jesus' death and the mystery they had heard about the Lord's body disappearing from the grave site. They were so "down" and consumed by the these mysteries that they didn't even recognize the Lord as He joined them walking. They seemed "blind" and unable to look unto Jesus, the Author and Finisher of their faith, as they attempted to run. Where was their faith, their courage, they excitement and joy? Jesus said to them, "O fools and slow of heart to believe all that the prophets have spoken: Ought not Christ to have suffered these things, and to enter into his glory? And beginning at Moses and all the prophets, he expounded unto them in all the scriptures concerning himself." (LK 24: 25-26)

After that, these disciples invited Jesus to eat with them. And when Jesus took the bread, broke it, and blessed it, their eyes were opened and they recognized Him. At that moment. He vanished. Now, they were so excited, they went seven miles back to Jerusalem to tell the other disciples. By communicating truth to them, Jesus had turned these discouraged, dejected, unprofitable, and "blind" disciples into productive and enthusiastic ambassadors for Him once again. We need to follow His example as we disciple others.

Involve Our People In Planning. The prophet Jeremiah assures us of God's vision & his openness to receive our input. "For I know the thoughts that I think toward you, saith the Lord, thoughts of peace and not of evil, to give you an expected end. Then shall ye call upon me, and ye shall go and pray unto me, and I will hearken unto you. And ye shall seek me, and find me, when ye shall search for me with all your heart." (JER 29:11-13). He tells us to ask, seek, and knock (MT 7:7).

He truly wants to hear our heart's requests. We, with wisdom from above, will want to hear our people's desires and to involve them in goal setting just as the Lord involves us. "Then saith he to his disciples, The harvest is truly plenteous, but the laborers are few; Pray ye therefore the Lord of the harvest , that he will send forth laborers into his harvest." (MT 9:37-38) Runners run best when they "see" the finish line. Disciples "kick hardest" when they see the goal set before them and when they perceive that they've contributed to set that goal.

Another behavior Christ left us as a legacy to emulate, in our roles as disciple-maker leaders, is **Developing A Heart** in disciples **For Serving Others**

MANTLE GARMENT – The mantle-wearing prophets knew what they were here to do (i.e. their service) and whom they served (i.e. their customers)

The wisdom that God gives is "full of good fruit" (JA 3:17). One of these is "goodness". PS 23: 6 declares that since the Lord is my shepherd, "Surely goodness and mercy shall follow me all the days of my life..." It's also a "fruit of the Spirit" stated in GAL 5: 22.

"Goodness" means that you want only the best for your people. As such, you will want to give them a heart for serving others because (as we have seen above) that will make them the "greatest" and will satisfy the depth of their soul. So, how can we do this? How do we get a heart in those we disciple for serving?

First, with our people we need to ask ourselves and agree upon, "What are our products & services? In whatever we do as Christians, we are about Father's business – the business of making disciples of all nations. Each of us has a role to play in making disciples. We don't all have the same function. Some plant seeds while others reap the harvest. Some are apostles – pioneering new works for the Lord.

Others are evangelists, who have the gift of witnessing for Him in an especially effective way. Some are missionaries – some with designated positions in the kingdom of God and others who by their words and behavior are missionaries to wherever they gravitate. Some are pastors – some with designated positions and others who are influential (like a father) in another's life. Some are teachers – some with the gift of teaching demonstrated by teaching a bible study, home group, discipleship class, etc. While, at the same time, all Christians teach by example and by their testimonies.

There are many other areas of ministry and the body of Christ matures as we "touch" one another's lives in many different ways (EPH 4:16). As we disciple others and help them determine God's calling on their lives to make disciples themselves, we need to identify specific products and services that are involved. For some the service may be administration and the product might be an organized ministry team. To another, the service might be helping and the product might be a less-pressured husband or wife more prepared to serve the Lord.

Jesus had both products and services. His products are transformed people – like you and me. His services are many. They include: salvation; maintaining our lives by his Lordship; setting us in a local church to serve one another (i.e. our internal customers); empowering us to reach the unsaved (i.e. our external customers); developing a heart in us for satisfying our heavenly Father.

To get a heart in our people for serving others, we also need to ask, "Who are our customers? Who do we serve? What are their names? We serve God first – that is always true. In addition, God leads us to serve others. As mentioned above, we could have internal customers (e.g. those we minister to in our local church or in our families) and external customers (e.g. those in the community's local government, hospitals, nursing homes, homeless on the streets, school children, people in our neighborhoods, those in our workplaces, etc.). Jesus' primary customer was His heavenly Father. He was always about Father's business (LK 2:49) "This is my beloved Son, in whom I am well pleased..." (MT 17:5) Besides "rating" Him, it was His Father that Jesus needed to show Himself to after the resurrection. "Jesus saith unto her, Touch me not; for I am not yet ascended to my Father..." (JN

20:17) Christ's secondary customers, of course, were all of us – the sick (i.e. sinners) who needed a Physician to save them.

We also need to equip our people for serving these customers effectively. They need your own and others' experience and example in a particular area. They need as much information and knowledge and ministry resources that are available. They need to know the basics from you (their mentor) of Bible study, prayer, worship, and fellowship. Our objective as disciple-makers is to give them competence and confidence in serving others. We need to teach them to manage "moments of truth" well. These moments are when their customers will be watching them ever so much closer than normal and evaluating their performance.

Every job has moments when customers evaluate the service they are receiving. In restaurants, we subconsciously rate service by such things as ambiance or the greeting of the hostess, or how our menus are presented to us, or whether our meal has the same size portion as the person with whom we're eating. Jesus had these moments of truth.   When the Pharisees tried to entangle Jesus in His talk, they sent the Herodians to ask Him, "Is it lawful to give tribute unto Caesar or not?"   The Father, Jesus' primary customer, might have been listening very closely for His Son's answer. "Render therefore unto Caesar the things that are Caesar's and unto God the things that are God's." (MT 22:21). I'm sure our heavenly Father was also very pleased with Christ's answer to the crowd that caught the woman in adultery.   How would Jesus fulfill the law requiring this woman's accusers to stone her, while at the same time undermine their attempt to force His hand and condemn a woman that was repentant over her sin? "He who is without sin among you", Jesus said to her accusers, "let him cast the first stone at her." One by one, from the oldest to the youngest, they went away until Jesus was left alone with the woman. Now, He who was really without sin, said to her, "Woman, where are thine accusers? Hath no man condemned thee?" She said, "No man, Lord." And Jesus said unto her, "Neither do I condemn thee: go and sin no more." (JN 8:7-11)   There were many other "moments" that Jesus managed well, pleasing the One He served. We must teach our people to manage their moments of truth well also.

Besides working with our people to decide what their products and services are; who their customers are; equipping them to serve competently and confidently; and, teaching them to manage moments of truth, we also need to help them determine how to measure success. Though quantities are often used to determine how successful we are in making disciples, it's really the quality of those disciples that matters most. Quality disciples make other quality disciples – "By this shall all men know that you are my disciples, if you have love one to another." (JN 13:35)

Perhaps an illustration will help us to build a heart in our people for serving others. If you were discipling someone who felt they were being called by God into teaching, here's what you might conclude are the products, services, customers, equipping resources, measurement criteria, and moments of truth:

- In general, as Great Commission teachers, **our product** is a transformed life – making disciples more like Christ. We keep our people focused upon Christ and the finish line (HE 12:1-2; PH 3:10-14). It's like what Jesus did on the road to Emmaus.
- In general, **our service** are as varied as it takes to make disciples – whatever they need (RO 12:1-2).
- Our **primary customer** is Christ. He is the One who gave some, apostles; and some prophets; and some evangelists; and some pastors and teachers..." (EPH 4:11) Other customers include other believers and unbelievers.
- **We equip ourselves and the Lord's disciples** for satisfying the Lord, other believers, and unbelievers by teaching them how and then helping them to discipline themselves to study the Word of God, Pray, Worship, and Fellowship with other believers. We also teach them how to deal with the "storms" of life.
- In general, we **measure success** by the standard of GAL 5:22-26, the fruit of the Spirit. If we have a class, we measure the degree of cooperation, camaraderie, and faithfulness in serving our customers (LK 12:35). A customer survey may help us. As teachers we always remember IS 55:10-11, especially when results are difficult to "see". "For as the rain cometh down, and the snow from heaven, and returneth not thither, but watereth the

earth, and maketh it bring forth and bud, that it may give seed to the sower, bread to the eater: So shall my word be that goeth forth out of my mouth: it shall not return unto me void, but it shall accomplish that which I please, and it shall prosper in the thing whereto I sent it."

- As a Great Commission teacher, we will have **"moments of truth."** One of these is <u>speaking the truth in love even when it is unpopular.</u>

PULL-DON'T-PUSH

The first behavior that flows from this value is **Building Up Our People's Self-Esteem (i.e. Encouraging and Empowering Them).**

MANTLE GARMENT – That evil woman Jezebel wanted to kill Elijah, who, with God's great power, had just defeated the prophets of Baal. Instead of Elijah maintaining faith that God could defeat her too, he ran from her. What would God do to Elijah for his lack of faith? God sent angels to him to feed and strengthen his exhausted prophet. When Elijah found himself in a cave, the word of the Lord came to him, " What doest thou here, Elijah?" God listened to his complaints and self-pity and tried to encourage him. Elijah hid his face in his mantle, ashamed of his performance (1KI 19:13). We don't overpower people into admitting mistakes – we offer a listening and learning opportunity to them so they can get their confidence back. God's primary interest was to get Elijah back to being productive for Him. God needed him to anoint Jehu to be king of Israel and Hazael to be king over Syria. He also needed him to anoint Elisha to be His prophet in Elijah's place.

The key message we need to send to our people is, "I believe in you." I believe you can do the work you are called to do. We can't say that, however, unless we've "empowered" them to do that job. This requires that we stay on the "empowerment track": GIVE DIRECTIONS, COACH, ENCOURAGE, and then EMPOWER. Jesus did this in LK 10 when He sent His disciples two-by-two into many cities. Jesus gave them directions. He had already coached them on how to do what He required – He was their example. He had allowed the disciples to speak for Him and cast out evil spirits. He had corrected their behavior until they themselves were confident. Then He trusted (i.e. empowered) them to go out by themselves.

When they make mistakes, most people already know it. They don't need to be reminded of that. Mainly they need a listening ear and a gentle but firm arm to lean on to help them learn from the experience and get them back on track. The secret is to cast out fear. "There is no fear in love; but perfect love casteth out fear: because fear hath torment. He that feareth is not made perfect in love." (1JN 4:18) This is what happened with Peter, when he denied the Lord three times. When Jesus met him at the Sea of Galilee, He knew that Peter was sorry for what he had done. Instead of rebuking him and reminding him of his "shortcoming", Jesus instead encouraged him to be productive in the kingdom. He first asked if Peter loved Him with a love that was selfless, desiring nothing in return (i.e. agape love). In addition, Jesus added, "Do you love me more than these (other disciples love me)?" Peter couldn't say he had a completely unselfish love. Peter said that he loved the Lord like a brother would love another brother (i.e. phileo love). Jesus said, "Feed my lambs." Jesus asked him again if he had an unselfish love. Peter answered it the same way. Jesus said, "Feed my sheep." Finally, Jesus asked Peter if he really had a brotherly love for Him. When Peter said he did, Jesus said, "Feed my sheep." (JN 21:15-19) Remember the "bruised reeds" of IS 42:3. Jesus doesn't break bruised reeds – neither should we.

The other behavior that proceeds naturally from embracing the "pull-don't-push value of the Lord is to **Recognize & Reward Good Performance.**

MANTLE GARMENT - When our people "take up the mantle" (i.e. take ownership and responsibility) they should be recognized. "He that receiveth a prophet in the name of a prophet deserves a prophet's reward." (MT 10:41)

Leaders look good because of "behind the scenes people" (EX 17:8-16). Great Commission disciple-makers need to never take for granted good performance on the part of their people. We need to remember to recognize and reward what he/she does right because that will be the performance that is repeated. We also need to "fit" the reward to the person. So we must know what will motivate them (JN 10:14). Everyone is different and incentives must also be different. Sometimes just saying "thank you" is enough. Other times something more tangible is needed. Often, giving someone challenging work to do for the Lord is a great way of showing your appreciation to them.

A day is coming day when we must all appear at the judgment seat of Christ "award ceremony" (2COR 5:10). He will reward us according to the things we did on earth to cooperate with the Holy Spirit in making disciples. Things done "in the flesh" (i.e. by the natural man) will be considered wood, hay and stuble. They will be burned up. What we did "from Him" (i.e. by His power) will be considered silver, gold and precious stones. We, like the Lord, should have award ceremonies. Also, Jesus isn't waiting until that award ceremony to recognize us. He rewards us every day in various ways. We should do the same. Here are some ways he rewards us regularly:

- He accepts us as we are while he shapes us into what he wants us to be.
- He gives us more responsibility and authority (i.e. empowers us).
- He gives us the desire of our hearts.
- He answers our prayers.
- He uses us more.

Chapter 7

A Race For Every Generation
The Three Spiritual Athletes Who Set The Pace

Adapted from *Changed Into His Likeness*, Watchman Nee, 1967

Lenny "Liv" Livright enjoyed the "campaign" trail of bringing Christ to others – especially giving his testimony of how the Holy Spirit brought him to Christ and also presenting Christlike leadership from the Word of God. In serving others and loosing life, he experienced the abundant life of which Christ spoke. But it didn't come without pain, sorrow, sacrifice, and discipline.

He had invited a young rebellious girl to stay temporarily in his home until she felt ready to return to her parents. Eventually she received Christ and was reconciled to her parents. That kind of success, however, was not always the case. After fifteen years of marriage, Liv found out that his wife was having an affair with a younger man whom he had welcomed into his home to help through alcohol withdrawal symptoms. His parents were Christians and he indicated to Liv that he had accepted Christ but needed help through his alcoholism. Liv and his wife went through Christian counseling and spent a lot more time together. His wife, however, left him with the children for six months to attend a Christian "live in" counseling center.

It seemed that their problems were over and for the next ten years all seemed well. The last five of those years, Liv and his wife had a home Bible study for singles every week. Two of the singles from the group went on to become pastors. Three or four others were married during that time. The Word of God was shaping Christian lives. Then it happened again. Liv's wife had an affair with another man about fourteen years younger than she. On their twenty-fifth wedding anniversary, Liv's wife left him and his daughter. This time she wouldn't receive any counseling and she wasn't returning to him. She eventually married the man. This happened just three months after Liv's mom, whom he cherished, died from a long battle with cancer.

Though Liv had done a lot of teaching by this time, his personal Bible reading and study was just for the lessons he taught. His personal prayer and worship time was "fit into his schedule" – he prayed and worshipped in his car on the way to work. When this tragedy happened, he decided to put God's schedule first. He humbled himself, got his priorities straight, and made quality time each morning early to be with the Lord in the Word and in prayer. And that discipline, which came about because of this pain and suffering, has continued. He's read the Bible through 10 times since then.

For eighteen months, day by day, week by week, month by month, Liv prayed earnestly that God would bring his wife back to him – hoping for one of many miracles he had seen God do over the years. He also communicated with his wife as often as she would permit. The experience left its mark upon Liv's life – there was nothing in his power that could change the situation – the disgrace – the eventual loneliness. But something strange was happening to Liv's adult Sunday School teaching. Instead of weakness, his class began to sense a new strength, a new power, a new control, a new dependence upon the One he taught about. Liv, himself, began to see deeper into the heart of his Teacher and to empathize with the suffering of others.

Finally one day while in prayer for the return of his wife, Liv sensed God saying to him, "Why are you looking at the closed door? Look at the open door." Liv knew God hated divorce but from then on sensed that his wife would not return. Liv kept teaching the weekly singles Bible study. One day a member of the group asked that he have it at her house. She invited two of her neighbors. One of them was a widow for ten years whose husband had died of cancer at forty-one. She never went to singles groups before but her children encouraged her to go just this one time. As Liv prepared to teach the Word, this widow said she thought that Liv and her had met. "Where do you come from?", she asked. They were born and raised in the same city about 5 miles apart. "What high school did you attend?", she asked. They had gone to the same high school. "What year did you graduate?", she asked. They had graduated the same year. "Did you graduate in January or June?", she asked. They had been in the same graduating class thirty years before but never knew each other. She looked a lot like Liv's mom. Two and half years later they were married. They found out that they had some of the same friends in common – their fathers played baseball together – and that Liv's neighbor as a teen was her close friend. Her handwriting was even like Liv's mom's handwriting!

It wasn't always easy to live as a divorced and remarried itinerant teacher of God's Word, but Liv knew this was God using a bad situation to make something beautiful out of it in His time. She encouraged Liv to "step out" for the Lord – to be that teacher God wanted him to be – so Liv taught the Word of God in many different denominations and Christian forums after that. She encouraged him to write books that have blessed hundred's – maybe thousands - of lives around the world. As a result, Liv's books made their way to India, South America, and many parts of the United States. She encouraged him so much that he nicknamed her "Encour". They lived and served the Lord together for many years – so that the later part of their lives was more fruitful for the kingdom of God than their early years.

A Race For Every Generation – Biblical Principles and Application

GETTING TO KNOW THE GOD OF ABRAHAM, ISAAC, AND JACOB

HE 12:1 - "Since we are compassed about with so great a cloud of witnesses, let us lay aside every weight and the sin that so easily beset us, and run with patience the race that is set before us…"

EX 3:6 - "I am the God of thy father, the God of Abraham, the God of Isaac, and the God of Jacob…"

God identifies Himself to us as the God of these specific three patriarchs because (as we run the Christian race), it is the combined experience of these 3 men that defines the race run by God's people on earth.

Here, we run across
Isaac's experience

Here, we run across
Jacob's experience

Here we run across
Abraham's experience

end   start

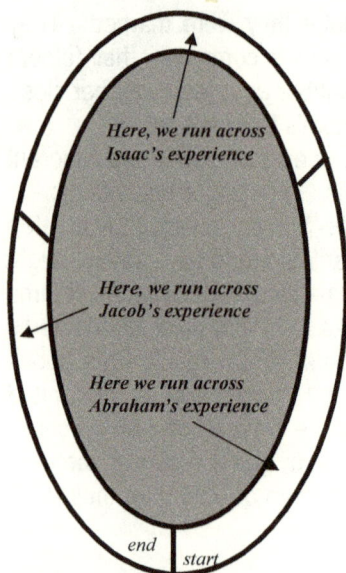

Abraham learned that God is the true originator, from whom all of His new creation comes. We all have to learn that we can originate nothing - 1Pe 1:3-5. God is the one who begins everything - He originates new life and preserves it. Nothing that originated from Abraham, including Ishmael - the son of his flesh - could serve God's purpose. We can bring an "Ishmael" on the scene at any time. But an Ishmael is only wood, hay, and stubble. He is of no use to God. When God does the work, it is gold, silver, and precious stones (the stuff that the New Jerusalem is made of). God is the Father – The Source.

Even after Isaac was born, Abraham needed to learn that God was still the Father. So He asked Abraham to take this precious gift of his son – that he could never have as a result of his own flesh but only by God's grace – and sacrifice him. Sometimes we Christians get the gift of a ministry from our Father. We too must remember that God is the Father both before and after the ministry is given. Remember in Genesis 1:31, "And God saw everything that He had made, and, behold, it was very good." Learning this lesson, we begin to be the "people of God".

Isaac illustrates the work of God in Christ towards us. We have "the adoption of sons" (Gal 4:4-6). God is also the Son, the Giver. Isaac teaches us that we have nothing that we were not given - nothing is by our attaining. Isaac did nothing that his father had not already done for him. He did dig wells – but they were the ones originally dug by Abraham and then refilled. He even

Us

Christ

sinned like his father – saying that his wife, Rebekah, was really his sister.

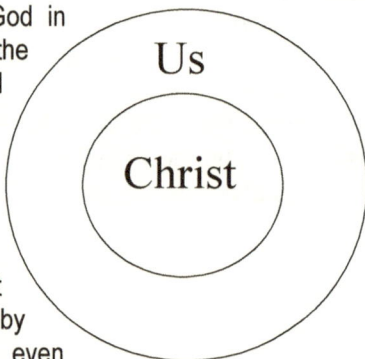

Isaac was born into wealth – he didn't get progressively more wealthy by working for it. We, also, do not progress/advance into wealth - we are born into it. We need only receive.

The two-fold work of God to give us all we need through Christ is given in John 15: 4-5. There Jesus says, "Abide in me, and I in you. As the branch cannot bear fruit unless it abide in the vine; no more can ye, except ye abide in me. I am the vine and ye are the branches. He that abideth in me, and I in him, the same bringeth forth much fruit: for without me ye can do nothing." Christ in us and us in Christ are the inheritance of the heir of God.

1COR 1:30 says that it is of God that we are in Christ. Being "in Christ" means that every aspect of Christ's past is ours – His death, resurrection, and His ascension to the right hand of God. They are all ours. Christ "in us" means that we have power to live life – overcoming life - the abundant Christian life with its great joy as well as its trials and suffering.

Jacob shows us that our "natural strength" so dominates us that enjoying God's inheritance depends upon the "touch of God" on that natural strength. As we saw in Chapters 1 and 2, before we come to Christ we are under the control of sin – that's called the "old man" in us. The old man was crucified with Christ (Ro 6:6). The natural man, however, remains in us. He competes with Christ in us and must be reduced to zero. God is compelled to eliminate any competitor to Christ in us. The experience of how this happens in Jacob illustrates the disciplinary work of the Holy Spirit in our lives. Because this is so prevalent in the Christian's life, the central lesson of God's dealing with Jacob is presented below.

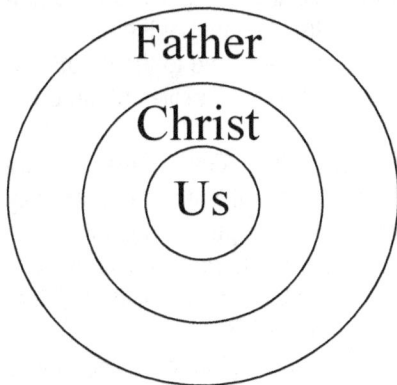

Father
Christ
Us

JACOB'S LIFE WITH HIS MOTHER and FATHER.

Jacob was a manipulator and cheat. Even from his birth, he tried to grab onto his brother Esau's heel to prevent him from being born first.

Before they were born, God told his mother, Rebecka, that she had two nations in her womb – and that the elder would serve the younger. Probably because Rebecka shared this with Jacob as a young boy, Jacob began to accomplish "God's will" – because it fit into his own plans very nicely – in his own way. He cheated his brother out of his birthright (GEN 25:31) and deceived his father into blessing him instead of Esau (GEN 27:19).

The result of Jacob's efforts was only that Esau felt himself cheated and determined to kill his brother, and Jacob had to leave home. The blessing he attained by cheating, he failed to realize – all he got was God's discipline. Clever Christians get a lot of that. Through discipline, God gave him the real blessing he had cheated to obtain.

JACOB'S LIFE WITH UNCLE LABAN – A TASTE OF HIS OWN MEDICINE

So Jacob's life of discipline began (GEN 28:10-22). At Bethel, which means House of God, God speaks to him in a *dream*. Since Jacob was trusting in his flesh – the natural man – God could not speak to him directly. God gives him the same unconditional promise that He gave to Abraham and Isaac – Verse 14 – "And thy seed will be like the dust of the earth, and thou shalt spread abroad to the west, and to the east, and to the north, and to the south: and in thee and in they seed shall all the families of the earth be blessed."

Jacob's answer in verses 20-21 sounds more like, "God, I'll make a deal with you." He said, " If God will be with me, and will keep me in this way that I go, and will give me bread to eat and raiment to put on, so that I come again to my father's house in peace; then shall the Lord be my God: and this stone, which I have set for a pillar, shall be God's house: and of all that thou shalt give me, I will surely give the tenth unto thee."

Besides his "business deal" with God, note that in verse17, Jacob was afraid of God and found this place "dreadful". The House of God is a terrifying place to those whose flesh has not been dealt with – because that's where God's power, order, holiness, and righteousness are revealed.

GEN 29:14-15 shows that God had prepared Jacob's uncle Laban to give Jacob a taste of his own medicine. Jacob thought he was going to have a "free ride" in terms of staying there, but in these verses we see his uncle change that staus after one month. He says to JACOB (in essence), "You can't stay here for free". He says it of course in a deceptive way. And so over the next 20 years, Jacob is deceived many times – He worked 7 years for Rachel and got Leah instead. He had to work 7 years more for Rachel. He had his wages changed 10 times. So Jacob went through the fires of discipline, tested and tried, but always with God's hand upon him – because God had promised to bring Jacob back home. We too are "hidden" in Christ when we are tried. We need to remember that God has also given us great promises as well – RO 8:28 – JN 14:1-3 – just to mention a couple.

GOD'S "TOUCH" ON JACOB'S NATURAL MAN

GEN 31:3,13. After 20 years, God speaks to him, "Return unto the land of thy fathers, and to thy kindred; and I will be with thee...." Jacob left that place and headed home and his uncle followed him. But God protected Jacob (GEN 31:24). When the testing has accomplished its purpose, God lets us go – and no man, not even a Laban, can keep us.

Something surely has happened to Jacob. We see in GEN 31: 51-53 that Jacob sacrifices to God. He had learned to recognize God's voice. Discipline has not changed him much but at least he has progressed to WANTING GOD! In the early years, he wanted GOD'S PURPOSE – because it fitted his desires. He had wanted GOD's PURPOSE BUT NOT GOD HIMSELF. Now he had some desire for God.

As Jacob went on his way, the angels of God met him and Jacob saw them. He called the place Mahanaim, meaning "two companies." God opened Jacob's eyes to see that just as he delivered him from Laban, He would deliver him from everyone else. It was as if God were saying, "the two companies were not you Jacob, alone, but always God's company with you." GEN 31:55 – 32:2.

Surely all of this was enough to make anyone – even this strong natural man – trust God. He had God's command to return home, God's promise of his seed being so numerous and every nation being blessed from him, God's protection from everyone, and the vision of God's heavenly host. No, all of this was NOT ENOUGH! Remember, God's grace does not alter the flesh – only discipline can do that.

So, instead of trusting God, Jacob sent a very insincere, flattering message to Esau (GEN 32:3-4). He had already forgotten God's call, His grace, and His protection. Jacob worried and questioned, "What does it mean that Esau was coming with 400 men?" Clever Christians have many worries. Schemers pile up troubles for themselves. Those who "think and contrive" instead of "trusting and believing", find themselves like Jacob, "Greatly afraid" and "distressed" (GEN 32:7). He was obeying God in going home, but he dare not leave the results of his obedience to God. That was too risky. How many of us obey God by the front door, and make preparations to retreat out the back!

Jacob was obeying God but trying to escape his brother. He devises a plan and divides the people with him into two companies (GEN 32:7). Jacob substitutes his Mahanaim for God's. There was one heavenly company and one earthly. Now there are two earthly companies. Then Jacob prays his first real prayer. (GEN 32:9-12). God's discipline has helped Jacob make some progress. In the early years, it was just scheming and bargaining – now it is scheming and prayer. How like many Christians he was: "Of course I must trust God; but to trust Him fully and completely is too great a risk." Jacob looked to God but also used all his wits and strength to make the most elaborate preparation just "to be sure".

It was on that night, that God met him. Jacob was left alone in a place called Penial. There it says he wrestled a man till the "breaking of the day". He wrestled in the dark. He didn't know who or why he wrestled. God uses light to expose to us the true motive of our life. He must bring us there so we can see that all we have boasted in and gloried in about ourselves is SHAME! So now it was that Jacob put forth his utmost strength. It was not Jacob who took the initiative to wrestle, it was God who came and wrestled with him to bring about his utter surrender. But it says of God that "he prevailed not." (Verse 25). Jacob had great natural strength – like us who employ all sorts of natural skills for our self-protection.

It was as if Jacob were saying to God, "I can do all things through my strength." "Is anything too hard for me?" This is quite different from when God announced to Abraham about his having a son at age 100 (GEN 18:14), "Is anything too hard for the Lord?" One day we must acknowledge defeat, confessing that we know nothing and can do nothing at all. Jacob had not come to that place in his life, so something more than discipline was needed. Discipline brought him to Peniel where God could meet him face to face. And it brings us to the place where God can touch us in a fundamental spot of our natural strength. God's method of dealing with the natural man is to weaken us so we cannot rise. God has His way of doing that with each of us.

Jacob was stronger than most of us. Had God used some other method to weaken him, it could have taken another 20 years. So when Jacob would not yield, God "touched him" in the strongest part of the body – the thigh. God will put in jeopardy what we are trusting in – or what we are most proud of. There must come a day when God dislocates that thigh, undoing our strength of nature. Our strong point might be quite different than Jacob's: It may be AMBITION to drive us on to greater accomplishments. It may be BOASTING to convince others of our greatness. It may be EMOTIONS to get whatever we want from people. It may be SELF-LOVE to boost our own self-esteem. Our mistakes vary. But generally all of them spring from one inner principle – and when all the symptoms point to one disease, that is our thigh. May God open our eyes to see the nerve center of our natural strength. When that is touched, there will be fruitfulness. (GAL 5:22-24)

One touch and Jacob was lamed. Dawn came and he said to God, "I will not let you go" Now Jacob was truly weak and so the Divine Wrestler could not leave him. Jacob depended upon Him. It's when our thigh has been touched that we can hold God the closest. 2COR 12:10 says, "We are strongest when we are weakest." With an abundance of natural strength, we are useless to God. With no strength at all, we can hold on to Him. Look at God's response to Jacob (GEN 32:28). To the world, this match showed Jacob was a loser. He was pinned, defeated, surrendered. But God said he had prevailed and would be called Israel – prince of God. This is what happens when our natural man surrenders, beaten, at God's feet.

Jacob only knew that God had somehow met him – and that now he was crippled. The limp is the evidence – not merely the witness of his lips. We are to look to God to do the work in us in His own way and time. The result will be visible in us and there will be no need to talk about it!

God is the God of Abraham, Isaac, and Jacob. As we run the Christian race, we will experience their experiences – and learn their lessons. God is (and must be) the Originator. Nothing we do in the flesh can please Him. Also, He is the Father both before and after our Isaac comes. God is the

Great Giver of everything – We are heirs with Christ of great wealth. We are born wealthy as Christians because Christ is in us and we are in Christ – that's all we need. In addition, God will "pin down" the natural man in us until the life we live is Christ. He will progressively weaken the "source" of our natural strength so our work is truly His own – so He produces through us gold, silver, and precious stones – not the wood, hay, and stubble of the flesh.

Chapter 8

The Test of Endurance
Practical Helps For Great Commission Believers

Liv had some wonderful role models who emulated Christ and helped mentor him.

Mr. Tract was a co-worker who considered his brightest moment the time when he could afford to have a Christian sandwich sign made. It had scriptures on it and Mr. Tract wore it around him as he witnessed and handed out tracts in lower Manhattan. Liv learned how to be content and how to serve the Lord with gladness.

Mr. Word went to be with the Lord at the age of 99. He got up early every morning and took a cab to work at a gas station till he was 95. He attended Liv's Sunday school class till he couldn't get a ride. Mr. Word would always share words to live by with Liv as they sat together in church. He taught Liv to love, appreciate, and study the Word of God.

Ms. Cross taught Liv to "cross himself out" every morning and be available for service.

Mr. Rich allowed his apartment, where he lived with his wife and three children, to be used to start a church. He was always encouraging Liv despite his poor circumstances. He showed Liv how to build loyalty and build up other people – and also how to pray.

Ms. Love lost a child in a horrible accident, her husband had a debilitating disease, and her grandson had an emotional problem. Her major concern – despite all that – was showing the love of Christ to others. She showed Liv how to speak the truth in love, how to put others first, and how to laugh in the Lord.

Mr. Friend mentored Liv in leadership. He didn't hesitate to admonish Liv to keep him on track and to warn him about making certain decisions for his life.

Ms. Wise helped to keep Liv as gentle as a dove but also as wise as a serpent concerning people using and abusing him.

Mr. Care's wife had cancer. He kept bringing her to one healing service after another until the Lord healed her. At 70 years old this loving servant of the Lord had no pension from the churches he had served over the years. But he kept preaching the Word, as well as visiting and comforting the sick. He taught Liv all about perseverance and love.

Ms. Sunday was more faithful than most in attending Sunday school. She showed Liv how everybody can learn and be creative with a little love and encouragement.

Ms. Persevere had a disabled child. This child required much patience and care. Despite this, she ran for her life God's way by serving the needs of others in and outside the church. She taught Liv what patient endurance really meant.

The Test of Endurance – Biblical Principles and Application

Every believer is commissioned by our Lord Jesus Christ to go and make disciples. He said, "All power is given unto me in heaven and in earth. Go ye therefore, and teach all nations, baptizing them in the name of the Father, and of the Son, and of the Holy Ghost: Teaching them to observe all things whatsoever I have commanded you: and, lo, I am with you always, even unto the end of the world." (MT 28: 18-20)

As we run for our life God's way, we must "lay aside every weight and the sin which doth so easily beset us, and…run with patience the race that is set before us…" (HE 12: 1). Runners use weights in practice to get ready for the race. It's harder to run that way but it "feels so good" when the weights come off for the real race. Weights are OK in practice, but only hold us back in the real contest. We are in a real race – not practice. Sin is a weight that prevents us from running our best. As we live the Christian life, we will sin. These sins could become like trying to run a race with an elastic band wrapped around our feet. God, however, knew this and provided a way to lift that weight so we can run patiently all the way to the finish line with His strength and endurance. "If we confess our sins, he is faithful and just to forgive us our sins, and to cleanse us from all unrighteousness." (1JN 1:9)

As Christians, we need to keep ourselves pure (1TI 5:22). Entering into a close relationship with evil will corrupt a Christian. Partnering in business or in marriage with an unbeliever is contrary to God's Word (2COR 6:14-15). Remaining pure under these conditions and trying to change the unbeliever could be compared to preventing a muddy river from polluting a clear stream when they meet. Now, having said this, it does not mean that we separate ourselves from unbelievers – on the contrary, these are the very ones who need us most of all. These are the ones (among whom we were a part) that Jesus came to save. He said that the "sick" are the ones who really need a physician. But He also said that though we were in the world, we were not "of" the world. So as we run the race with Christ as our Partner and Coach, we cannot at the same time run with the world (AMOS 3:3). We cannot serve two masters – God and the world.

We need to keep the channel between us and our heavenly Father and also our fellow runners continuously free from the obstructions that sin creates. Therefore, we must develop an intimacy with God that allows us to readily confess our sins to Him. This will keep us effective in reaching out and "touching" others – both younger believers and unbelievers. We need to realize that this is the only race in which spectators get in the race because of the way they see runners running! This is sometimes called "reproducing ourselves": "And the things thou hast heard of me among many witnesses, the same commit thou to faithful men, who shall be able to teach others also." (2TI 2:2). These "spectators", who are being molded by the Holy Spirit as they see our lives, are (among others) fellow church members, our children, grandchildren, coworkers, friends, students, team members, or our spouses.

Here are some practical ways to "step out" smartly and attract spectators to join with you in running for your life God's way:

The Unbeliever and the Young Christian

OPEN TO THE IDEAS OF OTHERS

We listen to the concerns, wants, and desires of young believers. Don't be afraid to meet their friends. We don't criticize the associations and habits of the old life. Instead, we become to them living examples of the abundant Christian life with its spiritual treasures and precious fellowships. We allow the Holy Spirit to change the young believer's fun and fellowship.

When leading someone to Christ, we try to understand them as a person without accepting or agreeing with the sin in their life. Instead of concentrating on what we want to say, we focus on the legitimate interests and concerns of the one we are trying to reach. We stand ready to help by listening and lovingly offering our best wisdom.

We befriend a new Christian and spend time with them. Listen proactively to them and let them express themselves. Remember the essence of Jesus' words in LK 7:47, "He whom I have forgiven much, loves Me the most." As long as it's not a sinful place, we need to go where they want to go – to be like Jesus when He went to Matthew's collection of tax collectors. We use these occasions, however, to minister Christ and allow the Holy Spirit to "work with those (including the new believer) who need a physician." He may use it to promote reconciliation like He did with the little (but big thief) tax collector.

BUILDING LOYALTY

We show young believers and those we are leading to Christ that we care for them before ourselves. We give them the time they need from us to have all their questions answered – or to pray through certain problems. We say, "Call me day or night." We assure that they get to church, Sunday School, Bible studies, and fellowships.

We warn them of those things that would hurt them – without being hypocritical (i.e. we are their best example of Christian living). This is similar to Jesus who warned Peter, "Get thee behind me Satan." Our attitude is that we have "beams" in our own eyes so we are gentle and loving when we try to remove the "speck" in our brother's eye. We fight, however, anything unfair, immoral, or abusive affecting him. We also find ways to give loving but firm discipline when required.

We are careful to teach the young believer the difference between what is scriptural and what might be just tradition of a particular church group. This prevents no extra "burdens" to be carried by the young believer.

We teach them the joy, peace, and thrill of the Christian life, as well as the struggles – we share from our own life's experience. We assure them that they have us as spiritual mentors (i.e. parents) – 1 COR 4:15 (feed, protect, and train) and JN 21 ("feed my sheep").

We patiently teach them how to become spiritually mature and equip them for living the Christian life – How to Study the Word, Worship, Pray, Fellowship, and Surrender themselves to serve the Lord in some area of Father's business.

BUILDING SELF-ESTEEM (I.E. EMPOWERING OTHERS)

We feed new believers the "milk" of the Word and don't expect more from the spiritually immature than we should. We are patient with them (2TI 2:24)

We encourage them to give their testimony (JN 9:25 - "...one thing I know, that whereas I was blind, now I see") for leading others to receive Christ. Use the pure channel of the young Christian in their exuberance and "first love" for Christ to draw others to Christ. Use the incorruptible Word of God to sow the gospel message in the hearts of others. Keep pressing home the need to "be fruitful and multiply." Show them how. Bring them with you. In this way we empower them for service.

We teach them how to study God's Word – not just to hear and read it. We need to empower them to make their own decisions and be guided by the Holy Spirit – not to depend upon us. Show them how to hide the Word in their hearts and use it for personal correction and making right decisions, testifying, and drawing people to Christ.

We spend time to build new believers in the faith. It may take twenty minutes to a couple of hours to lead someone to Christ. It make take, however, twenty weeks to a couple of years to get him on the track to maturity, victorious over the sins and recurring problems that come along.

GOOD COMMUNICATIONS AND PLANNING

We see to it that they have a clear understanding of the gospel. Remember, the person either is now or was very recently spiritually dead – blinded by Satan (2COR 4:3-4) to the Gospel. Give them the "heart of the Gospel - Christ died for our sins, was buried, and rose again the third day according to the scriptures (1COR 15:3-4). Why does a person need to believe the Gospel? First, because he's a sinner (RO 3:23). God hates sin and says that the wages of sin is death (RO 6:23). But RO 5:8 says, "…that while we were yet sinners Christ died for us…" And only Christ could have (ACTS 4:12). He was sinless, so He could pay the penalty for us. 1PE 2:24 says that He did so that we, being dead to sins, should live unto righteousness. His purpose was to make us the sons of God – to restore a right relationship between us and our heavenly Father. JN 1:12 says this happens by receiving Him. This matter of receiving means repentance not just intellectual assent (LK 13:3). "Behold", Jesus said, "I stand at the door and knock." What door? The door of our hearts. When you hear His voice, what do you do? Let Him in. Then 1JN 5:11-12 applies, "And he that has the Son, has life."

Just as Jesus involves His disciples in planning (i.e. "Ask…Seek…Knock…" also "Pray ye that the Lord of the harvest that He would send laborers…"), likewise we need to involve the young Christian or those we are leading to Christ, in our planning process. "We ask, "Where do you want to go?" "What do you want to do?" "What should be our goals over the next several months…this year?" As we do this, we need to show the new Christian what his real needs are. Each new believer will have different needs. Invite him to allow Jesus to take him on the incredible journey through his heart – especially emphasize what the young believer would serve the Lord in the dining room of his heart. Let him determine if his "appetites and desires" are material possessions, family, education, etc. OR "My meat is to do the will of him who sent me, and to finish his work." (JN 4:34)

BUILDING UNITY AND FAMILY

It's important to teach the young believer about the four "unities" of the Christian life:

- Unity with God. Through Jesus Christ, we have a right relationship with our heavenly Father. We are His children.
- Unity with brothers and sisters of our local church. The Scripture says that God has "set" us in the local body of Christ (1 COR 12:28). We are to love one another (RO 15:7); accept one another (RO 15:7); prefer one another (RO 12:10); bear one another's burden (GAL 6:2,5);

bear with one another (EPH 4:2); be members of each other (EPH 4:25); build up and encourage one another (RO 14:19).

- Encourage the new believer to experience this oneness by joining a small group fellowship or Bible study or prayer group.
- Remember the new believer's birthday, wedding anniversary, or other special occasions with a card or take them out with other believers.

- Unity with other Christian brothers and sisters who are not part of your own church. When Jesus prayed that believers would be one (JN 17:21), I believe He meant a visible unity that the world could see so that the world would know that our Father sent Christ into the world (17:23). We should encourage new believers to participate in cross-denominational prayer, evangelism classes, vacation Bible school, and on the lighter side in inter-denominational softball leagues, picnics, etc. Remember we are co- laborers with Christ and are all Christians in the work of evangelism. We ALL have the Great Commission.
- Unity with the "potential" members of God's family who have not yet accepted Jesus as Savior and Lord – those who haven't begun to run. Remember that God demonstrated His love to us in that WHILE WE WERE YET SINNERS Christ died for us (RO 5:8). We should encourage other believers to share their testimony with unbeliever friends, relatives, coworkers, and others of how God led them to Christ.

RATING PERFORMANCE WELL

Young believers and even those we are leading to Christ need to be mentored in a way that says, "We love you as a person; but we sometimes disagree with the things you do." The Scriptures teach us to admonish, correct and restore one another gently – to speak the truth in love. As we "point the finger" at these others, we need to be ready to accept feedback from them also.

We should encourage them to examine themselves against the standards that God has set for our lives. When they do that, we should encourage them to remember that God is "faithful and just to forgive our sins and cleanse us from all unrighteousness" (1 JN 1:9).

We should involve others in providing feedback to the young Christian – to give them "a circle of feedback" from various people interacting with them. Those providing this feedback might include the pastor, a deacon, a brother or sister in Christ, and those whom the young believer is serving (i.e. a nursing home resident or hospital patient or member of his/her Bible study group).

RECOGNIZING AND REWARDING PERFORMANCE

Be appreciative of what the young Christian or person you are leading to the Lord does. There is so little of this it seems that it will mean a lot. When he overcomes some trial/tribulation, show your pleasure with a note or by going out together – help him/her remember and treasure that special time.

Give the young believer who wants to serve the Lord some meaningful work to do. Encourage them, but don't "twist their arms" to do something. Also try to determine what motivates them, don't assume that what motivates you will also motivate them. As he/she matures, remember to increase responsibility and authority.

DEVELOPING A HEART FOR SERVING – CUSTOMERS

Watch for opportunities to show the young Christian or prospective Christian some courtesy or provide a service to them. Avoid getting a reputation for going to see these people just because you want to invite them to a church service.

Take him/her a batch of cookies or lend a hand with some house, yard, or school work. Call them on the phone, send email, or write a letter.

Take them to the hospital, nursing home, or witnessing on the street or at another church. Show them how to do it. Let them do it while you observe and lovingly provide feedback to help them.

Involve them as you teach, pray, worship, fellowship, and serve the Lord.

Teach them how believers become Christ's commissioned leaders, who are always about Father's business, as follows: Say that BELIEVER becomes a BELIEVER LEADER (or BELEADER for short) by removing the "I" in BELIEVER and living for Christ and others. Next, we remove the "V" in BELIEVER and stop vacillating between serving the kingdom of God or the world. If we do that, we have the word BELEER. Now, between the E's that stand for Earth and Eternity, put "AD" that stands for "Actively Disciple". You now have the word BELEADER – and you also have a believer who is exercising the commission that Christ gave us.

Let them decide for themselves in what area of God's business they want to serve. Teach them that everyone who runs for their life God's way is in the business of helping others onto the track and then helping them to finish well!

Brief Answers to Questions Asked By Young Believers Or Unbelievers

- **How can a loving God allow such cruel things to happen (e.g. the killing of innocent people)?** God made man with a free will – that's part of God's love for His creation. We are not puppets jerked up and down by God. That's important because man needs to choose to be God's child of his own free will – not because he must. Life is like a huge cruise liner in the ocean. God knows the destination, but men and women aboard make their free-will choices. Satan inspires people to do cruel things as they choose to obey him instead of God. As we witness, these people can become Christ's. As we take a stand for Christ, we take more of the "kingdoms of the world" (and Satan's) back for God – then there is less crime.
- **Why does God allow deformed or brain damaged babies to be born?** I believe it is because God wants other people to see them and consider how blessed they are – saying, "There but for the grace of God go I". In addition, He uses these babies – the weak things of the world – to confound the wise. I know a Down's Syndrome man who is 43 years old now. When I met him, he was about 20. He is loved by all – Christians and non-Christians – and he shows pure, unconditional love to everyone he meets. He is perfect.
- **Why didn't God heal my friend from cancer?** God's ways are not our ways. His thoughts are higher than our thoughts. Though we see things like this as tragedies, God may have something even more wonderful than we can imagine for the one who goes to be with him. Children who die are automatically with Him. When someone dies without receiving Christ, this should move Christians to "press toward the finish line" more intensely and love the unsaved more practically to draw them to Christ.

- **Why do good people suffer for what appears to be no reason?**
  For Christians the example is Christ. When we take a stand for Him,
  we make enemies. Jesus said that He came not to bring peace but
  rather division. He makes people choose Him as the only way to the
  Father or not choose Him. Some of the fallout of that decision impacts
  all Christians because we identify with Him.
- **Why didn't God just eliminate Satan in the Garden of Eden?** God
  created man to have fellowship with Him – to be His children and obey
  Him because they want to instead of being forced to. God was broken-
  hearted over the broken relationship between Himself and man. God
  has a plan. He sent Christ to show us His great sacrificial love for us.
  He gave us a way to satisfy the penalty for sin and restore the broken
  relationship. Man needs to choose Christ. He allows Satan to exist
  now (and even after the Battle of Armageddon) to allow man to make a
  choice. People must choose Him and eternal life or the temporary
  gratification in this life and eternal death. They choose either to
  receive in this life the "riches in glory by Christ Jesus" or the riches that
  the world system and Satan give.
- **Why do the wicked seem to get their way and prosper?** Just like
  Jesus was tempted in the wilderness by Satan, he also tempts many to
  "worship him" (i.e. all the wrong values and behaviors) in order to get
  power, influence, riches, and gratification of the human nature and the
  "old man". That's why the devil is called the god of this world and the
  power of the air.
- **Why did God allow the "old man" to put us in bondage to sin?**
  First, it was man – not God who put himself into bondage by
  disobeying God's command to refrain from eating of the Tree of
  Knowledge of Good and Evil. God then used that to show us how
  much He loves us by sending Jesus to die for us and crucify the "old
  man" with all of our sin. So man could then choose to be His
  voluntarily.
- **Why do some come to Christ when they hear the gospel and
  others don't? Does God stop some from receiving Christ?** God
  has foreknowledge of those who will come to Him – that's because He
  is God and knows everything past, present, and future. He wills,
  however, that all come to Christ (JN 3:16). The world and Satan seem
  to have a hold more on some than on others and they can't let go. I

have heard that most people come to Christ when they are young because they can accept change easier than older people. Jesus said that after people have tasted the "old wine" they like it better than the new, referring to the difficulty in many maintaining a "new wine skin" heart to accept new truth. Remember, however, that nothing is impossible when God's involved. It's also true that in some lives others have already toiled to make their "soil" more fertile for the Gospel than others.

- **How can I prove that Christ rose from the dead (and hence that He was and is the Son of God)?** The best book on this subject is "More Than a Carpenter" by Josh McDowell. First, the best way to prove it is by your own personal relationship with Him – how you were VS. how you are now. Remember that in the Book of Revelation they slew the dragon by the "blood of the Lamb and the word of their testimony." Here is more help:

  - **Theory – Jesus never died.** Answer – How could a bleeding, wounded, and eventually dead Messiah have inspired the fearful disciples to gain such great confidence to the point of giving up their own lives for Christ?
  - **Theory – The disciples moved His body.** Answer – It seems very strange that this band of fearful men and women could have overpowered or tricked the Roman soldiers. If that happened, why wouldn't the guards have hunted down the disciples, punished them, and produced the body of Christ?
  - **Theory – The disciples lied about the resurrection.** Answer – Why then didn't anyone produce Christ's body and show that it was a lie. That would have ended Christianity forever!
  - **Theory – The guards feel asleep and the disciples stole the body.** Answer – That would have been instant death for the guards. These were disciplined soldiers of Rome, who had conquered many people. That didn't happen with undisciplined men. The guards were probably shaken by the angels and either ran or fell unconscious.

- **Is it true that all Christians are supposed to prosper financially?** In the Sermon on the Mount, Jesus said, "Seek ye first the kingdom of God and his righteousness and all these things will be added unto you." He was referring to food, clothing and shelter – our necessities. As illustrations he used a lily and the birds – not kings and palaces. In fact, He said that even Solomon, with all his glory, was not dressed as well as the lily. In MAL 6: 10, God says that if we bring in the tithes, He will "open the windows of heaven and pour out a blessing that there shall not be room enough to receive it." I usually tell people who expect a lot of money because of that scripture to count all their blessings and see that it is really true – but not necessarily money. God does say in the next verse that He will "rebuke the devourer". In other words, He will help us to stretch the money and material blessings that we have – it won't seem like there are "holes in our pockets".

- **Why doesn't God just let someone in church win the lottery so all the church's needs will be met?** God wants everyone to be part of the process in meeting needs. In general, He wants everyone to contribute enough of their time, talents, strength, and money so that no need goes unmet in the church. It's the Acts 2: 42-47 solution. He also wants people to learn and build their character into Christ's through working for a living. Paul told the churches that if someone didn't work, they shouldn't eat. There's probably another reason for using this process instead of the lottery – the person who wins might just spend the money on themselves!

The Partnership Quiz For Brothers and Sisters In Christ

As Great Commission believers, we are called to make disciples. There's an area of disciple-making that is often forgotten. We've just finished discussing how we can help draw unbelievers onto the racetrack and how we can disciple him/her and other younger believers. Besides this group, however, we must remember that we are partners with the Lord and each other in helping each other mature as Christians. We are partners in the process of helping each other to be shaped into the image of Christ. The New International Version (NIV) of EPH 4:16 says, "From Him the whole body, joined and held together by every supporting ligament, grows and builds itself up in love, as each part does its work."

Test yourself on how well you're doing and, as you look up the scripture references, ask the Holy Spirit to help you in your "weak" areas. Rate

yourself this way: 1 – Strongly Disagree   2- Disagree   3 – Slightly Agree
4 – Agree   5 – Strongly Agree

- I bear with other Christians' personalities and habits by remembering "there but for the grace of God go I." (EPH 4:2) Remember the words of Jesus in JN 13: 14, "If I then, your Lord and Master, have washed your feet; ye also ought to wash one another's feet."
- Even when my brother or sister in Christ is clearly wrong in what they've said or done, I try hard to tell them in a way that keeps the unity of the Spirit in the bond of peace (EPH 4:2).
- I consider myself to be incomplete without the fellowship of my brothers and sisters in Christ and therefore speak the truth to them (EPH 4:25).
- I am kind to other Christians, by getting to know them well enough to be sensitive and not hurt them (EPH 4:32).
- I don't hold grudges. I am not hard-hearted. When I see they regret what they did, I forgive them in the same manner as God, for Christ's sake, forgives me (EPH 4:32).
- I submit myself as an instrument in God's hand in order to help my brothers and sisters in Christ – even if there's the possibility of being hurt or misunderstood by them. If that makes me feel uncomfortable and humble at times, I do it anyway (EPH 5:21) "…that we may be able to comfort them which are in any trouble, by the comfort wherewith we ourselves are comforted of God." (2COR 1:4)
- I am consistent and diligent in praying for other Christians (JA 5:16).
- I serve my brothers and sisters in Christ by faithfully using the gifts God has given me. (GAL 4:13, RO 12:4-9)
- If my brethren are overtaken in a fault, and seem to be sliding off the track, I don't ignore them but try to restore them, being sensitive to the Holy Spirit's leading (GAL 6:1).
- Though it costs me time, energy, and money, I bear my brother's or sister's burden. (GAL 6:2)
- My care for all the brethren is the same. In this way I really practice unity (1COR 12:25-26). Everyone in the kingdom of God should know what to expect – that help will always be there when he/she needs it.

- I try to prefer others over myself. I am in fellowship with others so I know their needs. And I am not just concerned about my own needs, but I make every effort to provide for the needs of others – even the lowliest of the brethren (PH 2:3-4, RO 12:16).
- I don't make "deals" with Christians or with God (like Jacob in GEN 28:20). I don't make others feel they "owe" me anything. And I don't let others make me feel that way about them. I remember, however, that I am obligated to love the brethren. (RO 13:8)
- I avoid judging my brethren. Instead, I'm careful not to make them feel they should do something that they really don't believe they should do. (RO 14:12-13, 23).
- I make a point to faithfully build up and encourage the brethren (RO 14:19-20). Also see Proverbs 10: 11, 20, 21 that have two constants: A righteous man and words that nourish and refresh others. Let us get a reputation like Job got, "Thy words have upholden him that was falling, and thou hast strengthened the feeble knees." (Job 4:4)
- I am not prejudice. I accept all brethren equally (RO 15:7, JA 2:1)
- I study the Word of God in order to be able to help instruct and even admonish my brethren when necessary (COL 3:16).

As we run this race and make disciples, let's also remember Jesus' words in MT 25:40, "And the king shall answer and say unto them, Verily I say unto you, Inasmuch as ye have done it unto **one** of the least of these my brethren, ye have done it unto me." Jesus never let the masses dissuade or discourage Him from helping people one by one. In LK 8:40, the multitude pressed about Him. Yet in verses 41-56, we read that He took time to minister to one man and one woman in need (i.e. Jairus and the woman with the issue of blood). Jesus calls us to do the same. Someone has said, "Those who want to help "everyone", often find themselves helping no one." Let's do what we can to help others - one person at a time. Let God then, as we mature in Christ, add others as we "seek first the kingdom of God and His righteousness."

Chapter 9

The Finish Line
Christ's Evaluation of Our Performance

One summer day, Liv was invited to address 60 pastors and leaders of a major denomination. It was exciting for him to think about what might result from giving "seed" to these "sowers" of the Gospel. That afternoon, the Virginia sun was burning brightly and Liv decided he would rest a while. As he contemplated what the Lord had given him to say, he fell into a deep sleep. He was launched into a heavenly realm where he stood with ten thousand times ten thousand and thousands of thousands. They were from every kindred, tongue, people, and nation. In the midst of these vast numbers of people stood a Judgment Seat and there in all His glory was Christ, Himself. At first, He was so bright that Liv couldn't tell it was Him; but it soon became apparent that this glorious person was his Lord. All the people praised Him and the sound of their cheers was deafening.

Liv joined in the singing and praising and then something very strange happened. Jesus looked at Liv. It seemed that the Lord's eye caught the eye of everyone at the same time. It was probably like what happened to Peter – after he had denied the Lord three times – when Jesus looked at him. The noise of the crowd seemed to hush and Liv could only see Christ's eye. The Lord's look must have only lasted a moment, but it seemed to Liv like a lifetime. He had experienced being heart-to-heart with the Lord, but now he was eye-to-eye.

Liv was lifted to spiritual heights unknown to him till now. He saw a stability -surpassing the tallest of earth's mountains; a strength – surpassing the combined force of the wind and ocean during a violent storm; a purity - surpassing the smallest of infants; a peace - surpassing the most tranquil waters; a deep, genuine care and concern – surpassing a mother's love for her nursing child; a joy - surpassing a father who receives back his rebellious son; and, a hope - surpassing the runner about the pass the finish line first.

With that look, it seemed that the Lord searched to see His own image in Liv. Though Jesus was looking in Liv for a reflection of Himself, Liv began to see himself reflected back to him. Liv began to see certain events from his life - they were opportunities he had missed to share the Gospel or to emulate Christ – they were times when he had worked for Christ in his own strength and not in His strength. Tears flowed over Liv's face as he viewed these things - for he saw them being burned up like wood, hay, and stubble.

Then Liv's eyes, as if controlled by a source outside himself, viewed more and more of the Lord's face – not just His eye. When he caught a glimpse of His mouth, the Lord began to smile with such warmth that Liv's tears were dried up instantly and he began to feel a certain glow about him. Then the Lord spoke to him and said, "Lov, enter the joy of your Lord and let me show you the pyramid of your life." When he heard the Lord call him "Lov", Liv was puzzled because the Lord had called him "Liv" in his dream so many years before. Knowing this, Jesus explained, "I called you "Liv" when you were searching to know Me. You were still living for yourself. You still had the "I" in the center of your life. But as you allowed yourself to be transformed, My name for you became "Lov", because you put Me and Others in the center instead of yourself!"

And then "Lov", as the Lord called him, was put into a pyramid with others whom he recognized and knew during his lifetime. They were all arranged into an upside down pyramid with Lov at the very bottom. The Lord then pointed to each one of these people and began to tell Liv what happened to them. The Lord began, "Do you remember this lady who was on the bus, who was almost ready to deny My existence? You ran after her, witnessed to her, and she received Me there in the parking lot. Do you remember? She became a Sunday school teacher and led many children to accept me also." And as He spoke those children – that Lov had never met - were added to the pyramid. "Remember this young man in your singles' group who became a pastor? He got a church in the inner city and he was put in charge of inner city ministry on the United States East coast. He made disciples who also went on to bring My Gospel to many inner city people." When He said that more people that Lov never met were added and the pyramid got even bigger. Then pointing to a group of people who were with Lov in the pyramid, the Lord said, "Do you remember these sixty people who accepted Me during the lay witness mission that you led? They each brought one more to me." And more people were added to the pyramid.

The Lord continued to tell him about the young soldier, who he had helped find his way back to Christ, the lesbian, who had accepted Him and became a Sunday school teacher, all the members of Lov's Sunday school classes, workshops, and seminars. There were many that Lov had touched that he was unaware of – some were children of parents he had helped stay together – others were people he had prayed for unceasingly, not knowing any of the results.

As Lov looked at everyone in the pyramid above him, he remembered what the Apostle Paul had told the Thessalonians, "For what is our hope, our joy, or the *crown* in which we will glory in the presence of our Lord Jesus Christ when he comes? Is it not you? Indeed, you are our glory and joy." (1 TH 2:19-20 NIV). He realized that the Lord had created a *crown of rejoicing* people all around him!

When the Lord finished speaking with Lov, he noticed that he was not at the very bottom of this pyramid. Esther, the woman who led him to Christ, was under him. And he was only a small part of her pyramid. Under her was another, and another further down, and that continued further and further downward. At the very bottom of the pyramid, with an uncountable number in the pyramid, was Christ. He said, "Do you remember when I told you that if you would be the greatest in My kingdom, you should be the servant of all? I told you, "Whosoever desires to be first among you, let him be your slave – just as the Son of Man did not come to be served but to serve, and to give his life a ransom for many." Lov realized that Jesus was First and Last – that He was the Source as well as the Finish Line of his faith. But there was something even below Christ. Lov realized after a while of straining to see that at the very bottom of the pyramid was the image of a broken heart – it was God's broken heart! But His heart was healed!

Suddenly, Lov felt another crown upon his head and the Lord said, "Behold your hope, and joy, and crown of rejoicing. Are not these people, to whom you ministered, who are now in My presence, your hope, joy, and crown?" Then without delay Lov cast that crown at the Lord's feet and these words fell effortlessly from his lips, "You alone are worthy, O Lord, to receive the glory and honor and power." Immediately the space around Lov became brilliant with light. And he remembered what Daniel had said, " They that turn many to righteousness shall shine as the stars for ever and ever." (DAN 12:3).

Then Lov heard a voice coming from the throne of God saying, "Praise our God, all you His servants, and you who fear Him, both small and great." And he heard once again the thundering of the great crowd saying, "Alleluia, for the Lord God Omnipotent reigns! Let us be glad and rejoice and give honor to Him for the marriage supper of the Lamb is come, and His wife has made herself ready!" Then Lov and the others were arrayed in fine linen, clean and white, which represented all the righteous acts of the millions in Christ's presence.

When Lov awoke, he fell to his knees and rededicated his life to Christ. He asked forgiveness for not using every opportunity the Lord had given him to share Christ with others; and also for the times he "lived by flesh" rather than living by faith and trust in Christ. He wanted more than ever before to tell people about Him – His stability, strength, purity, love, joy, peace, and hope – to tell Christians about their appointment with Him at the Judgment Seat. He started by telling the pastors that day and they went on to sow that seed in many other hearts. Lov will meet them all on that great Judgment Seat day in his crown of rejoicing!

The Finish Line – Biblical Principles and Application

"Know ye not that they which run in a race run all, but one receiveth the prize? So run, that ye may obtain. And every man that striveth for the mastery is temperate in all things. Now they do it to obtain a corruptible crown; but we an incorruptible (one)." (1COR 9:24)

God gives us many new starts – there are many "start lines" in the Christian race. Whenever we stumble and fall (i.e. when we fall short of God's expectations of us), we confess our sin to Him and because Christ has already paid the penalty for that sin, we get a new start. That new start line isn't back at the beginning, however, it's right where we stumbled – we keep going forward from there.

Yes, there are many start lines as we run for our life God's way, but there is only one finish line. It's at the Judgment Seat of Christ where all

Christians together must appear. "For we must all appear before the judgment seat of Christ; that every one may receive the things done in his body, according to that he hath done, whether it be good or bad." (2COR 5:10) At the finish line, there will be crowns given as rewards for what we did to cooperate with the Holy Spirit here on earth. These crowns will go to those who, through the power of the Holy Spirit, build "gold, silver and precious stones" upon the foundation of Christ. To those who work in their own strength, those works will be burned up and considered "wood, hay, and stubble" (1COR 3:11-15).

There are five crowns given in the Word of God as follows:

- "Crown of life" for those withstanding tribulation (REV 2:10)
- "Crown of glory" for elders, pastors, and leaders who have oversight of God's flock (1PE 5:1-4)
- "Crown of rejoicing" for faithfully witnessing (1TH 2:19)
- "Crown of righteousness" for those who long for Christ's return (2TI 4:8).
- "Incorruptible crown" for victors of the daily spiritual struggles (1COR 9:25)

In REV 4:10, we have a picture of the twenty-four elders having crowns on their heads. This means that the Judgment Seat of Christ had taken place. They took their crowns and cast them at the foot of the throne saying, "Thou art worthy, O Lord, to receive glory and honor and power: for thou hast created all things and for thy pleasure they are and were created." So we, likewise, who receive crowns will cast them at the feet of Christ. That's why when Christ returns (with us) in REV 19:12, He has on His head "many crowns."

So then, if we don't wear the crowns we receive at the Judgment Seat of Christ, what do we wear throughout eternity? DAN 12:3 has the answer. It says, "And they that be wise shall shine as the brightness of the firmament; and they that turn many to righteousness as the stars for ever and ever. We won't have crowns. We'll wear a mantle of light – similar to the Mount of Transfiguration light Christ showed to Peter, James and John. I believe the degree of radiance – like different stars shine brighter than others – will be based upon our faithfulness to follow the Holy Spirit's guidance on earth.

Before discussing this finish line any further, let's step back and review some things about this Christian race. As we have said, every Christian is a spiritual athlete. We are running for our life God's way. At first we were influenced by the "roar of the crowd" – the world, flesh, and the devil. We were on the broad track that was leading us to spiritual death. The Father's heart was broken because we, whom He had created to enjoy His fellowship, had an estranged relationship with Him because of sin. He sent His Son, who took upon Himself the form of a servant and was made in the likeness of men. He humbled Himself and, as an obedient Son, became the sacrifice for our sins that satisfied the Father. All of us who receive Christ are then "born-again" (i.e. born from above) by the Holy Spirit, who takes up residence within us. He sets us into the kingdom of God, which is both invisible (i.e. within us) and visible (i.e. in the form of the church).

Even though we are born-again, however, we find that the old values and behaviors that we acquired from the "roar of the crowd" continue with us. Over time we experience a transformation of these values and behaviors. We find the natural man in us, who competes with Christ in us, being reduced to zero – wrestled to the ground. This happens as we discipline ourselves to regularly study the Word of God, worship Him, fellowship with other believers, pray to our Father, surrender ourselves for His service, and by suffering trials/tribulations with His companionship and comfort.

By waiting upon the Lord to continually renew our strength, we run with patience and endure the "muscle aches" that of necessity come with long distance running. We maintain a portrait of the Lord before us. We don't just run for Him but from Him – He must do the work because anything done in our own strength (i.e. the natural man) can't satisfy Him. We *see* Him as our Inspiration (i.e. the Great Initiator of our faith), our Role Model, who's already run this race, and our divine Coach, who first teaches us how to run and then perfects us so we run well.

We are gently drawn onward by the Holy Spirit, who is always there reminding us of the race we are running:

- Because our enemy Satan is a liar and attempts to deceive Christians concerning what the real abundant Christian life is all about, the Holy Spirit asks, "What track are you on?" The "great career track?" The "ego building track?" The "material possessions or investment track?"

"Or are you", He reminds us, "on the high-calling track?" This is the narrow track – the course that's marked out by the example of Christ and leads to being shaped into His image. (PH 3:14)

- The Holy Spirit asks, "Is Jesus Lord of your life? Does He own the deed to your heart or is He just a guest there?"

- "What equipment are you wearing? Is it the armor of God that includes having "our feet shod with the preparation of the gospel of peace"; or are we wearing shoes with pointed tips that hurt our fellow runners?"

- The racetrack is full of obstacles – many peaks and valleys – many things that cause runners to stumble, scrap their arms and legs. The Holy Spirit reminds us that Jesus never leaves or forsakes us. He will not let us go through any suffering without Him. He's the one who asks us to come unto Him when we labor and are heavy-laden, to learn of Him, because He is meek and lowly of heart and will give us rest.

- The Holy Spirit asks us, "How are you running – by faith or by sight? Without faith it is impossible to please him: for he that cometh to God must believe that he is, and that he is a rewarder of them that diligently seek him." (HE 11:6) He reminds us that "all things work together for good to them that love God, to them who are the called according to his purpose." (RO 8:28)

- How are you moving? Are you crawling, walking, or running when it comes to Christian growth? Runners kick hardest when they "see" the finish line. You may be crawling and not running well because you have a "fuzzy" view of the finish line.

- Has the Holy Spirit ever asked you about who wins this Christian race? Do you try to beat me to the finish line? Do Christians compete with each other to win? No, that should never be the case. This is a team race where we all win together! We finish the race together and we are always about Father's business to help one another finish well! "Even when we were dead in sins, hath (God) quickened us together with Christ (by grace ye are saved); And hath raised us up together, and made us sit together in heavenly places in Christ Jesus" (EPH 2: 5-6)

- Whenever I'm reminded of "who wins" and helping each other win, the Holy Spirit reminds me about the "cloud of witnesses" in HE 12: 1. Who are the people that are the great cloud of witnesses in our lives? Is it just the Bible heroes of the faith? I don't believe they are the only heroes. When you're sitting in church with brothers and sisters in Christ, look around you. You'll find heroes of the faith there too. As "the Lord went before them by day in a pillar of cloud to show them the way" (EX 13:21), God also uses us Christians to help show one another the way as we faithfully study and share His Word.

- The Holy Spirit always wants us to remember the Prize for which we're running. Is it heaven? Is it to prosper here on earth? Is it to get the best mansion in heaven? Is it to get one of the five crowns? No, it's none of those things. The Prize is Christ – to be like Him – "to know him, the power of His resurrection and the fellowship of his sufferings" (PH 3:10). Jesus is the Prize of the high calling of God!
- Running the race looking backwards doesn't work. Past accomplishments can become an anchor. We can be guided by the past – like a rudder. Better yet, I want to keep my eyes forward and my body straining toward the marked out track. "...but this one thing I do, forgetting what is behind, and reaching forth unto those things that are before, I press toward the mark for the prize of the high calling of God in Christ Jesus." (PH 3: 13-14)

So, do you see the finish line? What does it look like to you? Once again, the finish line is at the Judgment Seat of Christ. It's not when we die. It's when we all appear together at that place. It happens after what is called the "rapture of the church". "The Lord himself shall descend from heaven with a shout, with the voice of the archangel, and with the trump of God: and the dead in Christ shall rise first: Then we who are alive and remain shall be caught up together with them in the clouds, to meet the Lord in the air: and so shall we ever be with the Lord." (1TH 4:16-17) Can you see the billions – like the stars in the sky – gathering before Christ?

So, brother in Christ, do you see the finish line? Do you see yourself carrying another brother that you helped overcome his alcohol addiction, or his anger, or whatever other sin was a weight that dragged him down in the race?

Sister in Christ, do you see yourself arm-in-arm with other sisters who needed your phone calls, visits, and prayers to overcome the pressures of life?

Pastors who embrace the values of the cross of Christ as a good shepherd will be surrounded by many they don't know. These strangers will thank the pastors for their great love and care. The pastor will say, "When did I show you love and care?" They will answer, "When you were a Christlike role model and faithfully preached to my relative, friend, or neighbor – because they then shared your message and themselves with me as you taught them."

You faithful teacher will cross that finish line with kids and adults you don't know along with your Sunday School or Bible study class. You overcame your own insecurity about being a teacher and trusted Jesus. You emulated Christ. You taught your people to lead others to Christ and now you see the results.

You deacon finish well with the parents, friends, and relatives of someone in your congregation because you remembered to faithfully keep them in prayer after you heard a prayer request shared at church.

You single-person finish arm-in-arm with those you faithfully fellowshipped and served with. You hear, "Well done thou good and faithful servant."

You mother and father finish with your kids. And you hug the Sunday School, Bible study teacher, or youth leader who led them to the Lord and gave them those solid Christian foundational values.

Don't be the Christian who finishes by the "skin of his teeth". He finishes rather empty-handed and regrets all the missed opportunities to "touch" and help others! There will be many tears at the Judgment Seat of Christ – let them be tears of joy – not tears shed for miserably missing ministry.

How much more time do you and I have to run this race? Only God knows. We must run well, help others finish well, and keep our eyes on the finish line.

"For we must all appear before the judgment seat of Christ; that everyone may receive the things done in his body, according to that he hath done, whether it be good or bad."

- 2COR 5:10

Chapter 10

The Victory Lap

Lov Livright and his wife, Encour, retired from their secular jobs and went to work for the Lord full time. Whenever or wherever the Lord would open a door, the Livrights would be ministering there. Lov appreciated so much being able to instruct and "touch" the lives of other Christians – even to make some small contribution to their becoming mature disciples.

As he grew closer to the finish line of faith, Lov's thoughts turned sharply to the abuses he saw in the Body of Christ – especially those things that caused division. One of the most important scriptures the Lord had imprinted on his heart was John 17:21. There, before His crucifixion, Jesus prayed to His Father about all His disciples, "That they all may be one; as thou, Father, art in me, and I in thee, that they also may be one in us: that the world may believe that thou hast sent me."

Lov thought how important it was that all Christians – The Body of Christ – the Church – the kingdom of God – maintain the unity of the Spirit in the bond of peace (Eph 4:3). Because by reflecting the image of Christ to the whole watching world, people would believe that God sent Christ and accept Him.

He remembered Jesus judging the seven churches of Revelation (Rev 2 and 3). One had become so active – working in its own strength rather than in the power of the Holy Spirit – that it lost its First Love. Lov thought, "That church needs to be reminded that all we can do is set the sail, but God provides the wind." Another church thought it was poor because it didn't have many material possessions – but it was really rich with the gold that comes from having their faith tried in the fire of affliction (1 Pet 1:7). Another church was heretical allowing doctrines of devils. Jesus said that

He knew where Satan's seat was in that church. Lov thought, "They need to know when you give Satan an inch, he becomes a ruler." Another church was tolerating a lying prophetess. Not only were they stretching the truth but they also had serious moral and spiritual compromise. Another church had a better reputation than they deserved. Another was lukewarm and self-satisfied.

Lov couldn't help feeling that the attitudes and behaviors of those Revelation churches were in the Church today. In the 30th year of running for his life God's way, Lov, regrettably, saw that the attributes of those churches remained in him and also in many others who call themselves Christians. He asked Jesus to take him deeper into the Book of Revelation. He noticed that the Lord was warning those seven churches and giving them time to better prepare for His return. The Lord, he saw, had four main messages for those seven churches:

1. Before He gave each church His judgment about them, He always gave them a picture of Himself. *He was telling them (and us) to always keep who He is in the center of our hearts and minds.* For example, to the Philadelphia church He introduced Himself as, "...he that is holy, he that is true, he that hath the key of David, he that openeth and no man shutteth; and shutteth and no man openeth..."

2. He told every church that *He knew their works*. This could be reassuring but for some of us it should be disconcerting too! The Lord knows us inside and out. He knows when we get off track and run in the wrong directions – how we ambush one another with anger, jealousy, deceit, immorality, slander, unforgiveness, pride, stealing, and betrayal.

3. He told four of the seven churches to *repent*. "If we confess our sins, he is faithful and just to forgive us our sins, and to cleanse us from all unrighteousness." (1John 1:9). Lov resolved to change the wrong beliefs, attitudes, and behaviors he saw in himself. He also committed to the Lord that he would take his stand against such things in the Church.

4. He told all the churches to *overcome*. The Lord reminded Lov of how we can overcome. God told Joshua as he took charge of God's people, "There shall not any man be able to stand before thee all the days of thy life: as I was with Moses, *so I will be with*

thee; I will not fail thee, not forsake thee. Be strong and of good courage for unto this people shalt thou divide for an inheritance the land...Only be thou strong and courageous...Be strong and of good courage; be not afraid, neither be thou dismayed: *for the Lord thy God is with thee whithersoever thou goest."* (Josh 1:5-9). Lov recalled that Jesus also said that *He would never leave nor forsake us* (Heb 13:5) and that we could *do all things through Christ who strengthens us* (Phil 4:13).

With the Holy Spirit in us, we <u>can</u> in deed *(and must)* overcome and by unity with our brothers and sisters in Christ witness to a dying world that Jesus Christ is the Way to eternal life.

In his latter years, Lov's heavenly Father assured him that He was always in control. He would be faithful to use every circumstance of Lov's life to accomplish His will – both in Lov and through him. Lov entrusted himself to God's ultimate, always loving purposes. Knowing that he was really completing the work His heavenly Father gave him to do was like nourishment to his soul.

> Together, let's run for our life God's way.
> Seek His kingdom –stay on track - not stray.
> Press toward the mark on the "high-calling" track.
> Set our hands to His plough and never look back.
>
> Make Him Lord of our heart – our sin set aside,
> As we run by His side – stride for stride.
> God put us in Christ, cleansed and empowered
> And our life at His throne can never be soured.
>
> Model His values. Show others His behavior.
> Show them how Christ is our wonderful Savior.
> Then we'll see them at Christ's awesome Judgment Seat,
> Our joy and our crown, soon in heaven we'll meet.

> \-   Lov Livright

The Victory Lap – Biblical Principles and Application

Have you ever watched what the winner of a race does just after running through the finish line? If it's an Olympic contest, with many nations represented, there always seems to be someone prepared to hand the winner his nation's flag so he/she can carry it around the track in victory. They have "center-stage". For a brief moment in history, the winner seems to be at the center of the universe. All alone now, with the competition left back at the finish line, the victor trots victoriously around the track. All the TV cameras and every eye from the "cloud of witnesses" are fixed upon the winner. Praises ring loud at the winner's great accomplishment.

In a sense whenever we run as a Christian, we are running a victory lap because Christ has won the victory for us over sin and death. However, God has provided another type of "victory lap" for His people and for Himself. He describes it in The Book of Revelation. Let's very briefly look at this book. The following illustration helps us understand the "key" to unlocking its message.

remember...

The key to unlocking the Book of Revelation is Gen 41:25-32. Joseph interpreted Pharoah's dream. The dream was doubled but it was one because God would soon bring it to pass. In Rev 22:6,7,12,19 there is a reference to this revelation happening quickly. The Book of Revelation is doubled but it is one. The Seals & the Trumpets tell the whole story - so do the angel messengers and the vials.

Other key points: Jesus rates churches - not just people (Rev 2&3). We, like the elders in Rev 4:11, will cast at Jesus' feet the crowns we receive at the Bema Judgment. We will carry through eternity the Mt of Transfiguration glory light of Dan 12:3. We return with Christ and become His mantle of tiny lights (Ps 104:3).

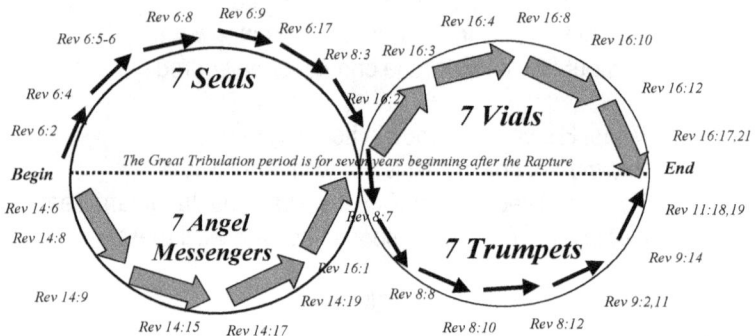

In REV 10: 1-11, John sees a mighty angel who has his right foot upon the sea and his left foot upon the earth. This angel has a "little book" opened in his hand. John is instructed to go and take the little book out of the angel's hand and to eat it. I believe it was this Book of Revelation because the angel told him, " Thou must prophesy again before many peoples, and nations, and tongues, and kings." (Verse 11) The book tasted sweet in John's mouth but was bitter in his belly. The Word of God is pleasant to the taste because it tells us about the blessedness and final victory for Christ and us. But it is bitter because we hold values that arouse the world's wrath and bring us persecution, suffering, and even death. And also because the Word declares the terrible trouble God will bring on those who reject its message.

The return of Christ is an event that those running the Christian race have awaited with great anticipation since our Lord ascended to the right hand of our Father. We are told in 1TH 4:13-17 that He "shall descend from heaven with a shout, with the voice of the archangel, and with the trump of God: and the dead in Christ shall rise first: Then we which are alive and remain shall be caught up together with them in the air: and so shall we ever be with the Lord." The church – the visible kingdom of God – is removed before God's wrath is poured out on the earth over the next seven years.

As we have said before, we must all then appear before the Judgment Seat of Christ. In REV 19:7, we rejoice because "the marriage of the Lamb is come, and his wife hath made herself ready. And to her was granted that she be arrayed in fine linen, clean and white: for the fine linen is the righteousness of the saints." Knowing our Lord, He will serve us at that banquet – as much as we will want to serve Him, then as now, we shall never be able to "out give" the Lord. And immediately after this wondrous "love feast", we swiftly find ourselves ready for battle. John sees heaven opened (REV 19: 11-21) and Christ, with many crowns, is seated upon a white horse. His name is called Faithful and True, the Word of God. On His thigh is written, KING OF KINGS and LORD OF LORDS. And we, described as "the armies of heaven upon white horses clothed in fine linen, white and clean", follow Him back to earth for the battle of Armageddon. John records that he saw the beast (i.e. Antichrist) and the kings of the earth, and their armies gathered together to make war against Him that sat on the horse and His army.

Every eye shall see Him and His entourage. We will be all aglow with the Son of Righteousness leading and many billions of smaller lights, like the stars of the universe, flowing behind Him forming His mantle. Then what God told Abraham, Isaac, and Jacob about their descendents being as innumerable as the stars of heaven will become literally true. Remember His words to Abraham, "Look now toward heaven, and tell the stars, if thou be able to number them: and he said unto him, So shall thy seed be." (GEN 15:5).

Rev 19:15 then says, "And out of his mouth goeth a sharp sword, that with it he should smite the nations: and he shall rule them with a rod of iron: and he treadeth the winepress of the fierceness and wrath of Almighty God." He casts the Antichrist and the false prophet into the lake of fire burning with brimstone. And Satan is chained up. Our Lord will then separate the nations as He describes in MT 25:31-46 and His thousand-year reign begins on earth with us ruling and reigning with Him.

So is this procession from heaven the "victory lap"? That's just the beginning! The real victory lap happens after the thousand years are over. The victory lap is called "The New Jerusalem". It's the future home for all of God's people from where we will rule and reign with Him. I like to call it "Honeymoon City" because God and us will dwell together and we shall see Him face to face forever. "...the throne of God and of the Lamb shall be in it; and his servants shall serve him: And they shall see his face; and his name shall be in their foreheads. And there shall be no night there; and they need no candle, neither the light of the sun; for the Lord God giveth them light: and they shall reign for ever and ever." (REV 22:3-5) It's "Honeymoon City" also because the angel who was showing it to John told him that this city was prepared as a bride adorned for her husband (REV 21:2).

My favorite name for it, however, is "Showcase City" because – like the winner of the race who runs the victory lap - God will have us on display for the whole universe to see the glorious and redemptive work of Christ. The crowds that once shouted for us to glorify "self" and follow the world, the flesh, and the devil, will be gone. In their place will be a "cloud of witnesses" throughout the universe who will constantly bask in the light of

"Showcase City". They will shout the praises of God and His Christ as they are eternally reminded of God's awesome, magnificent victory!

How could a city be "adorned" to be a bride? And how could it be a showcase? Let's look at the New Jerusalem. The church is housed there – all the born-again believers from all time. They adorn its streets. We shall be shining like the stars in the firmament (DAN 12:3). The degree of radiance will be determined at the judgment seat of Christ as we have already mentioned. In a way, we'll be like the precious stones that form the foundation of the City (REV 21:19-21). Precious stones that have been cut and shaped in the "heat" of this wondrous race our Father, through Christ, has given us to run by the power of the Holy Spirit. The names of the twelve tribes of Israel, the descendants of those fore-runners Abraham, Isaac, and Jacob, are inscribed at each of the twelve entrance gates (REV 21:12). And each of these gates were made of a *single pearl* (REV 21:21) – like "the pearl of great price" Jesus spoke of – which represents Christ Himself. The only way into the City is through Christ – the Entrance. "…the kingdom of heaven is like unto a merchant man, seeking goodly pearls: Who, when he had found *one pearl* of great price, went and sold all that he had, and bought it." (MT 13:45-46)

The foundations of the City have the names of the Lamb's twelve Apostles inscribed there (REV 21:14). And the streets are of purest gold like transparent glass (REV 21:21) – gold that Peter said was the precious faith of believers when it was tried with fire (1PE 1: 7). Finally, this City has "the glory of God: and her light was like unto a stone most precious, even like a jasper stone, clear as crystal." (REV 21:11) It was like a great glass case that contained the precious jewels of the Lord being displayed for the entire universe for ever and ever as a final victory lap of those who ran for their life God's way.

Some might ask, "Who in the universe will be there to see this great display – the Bride of the Lamb – the City of God's precious love?" Who will be cheering the Victor and victors? We know that the angels will be there, but who else? "And the nations of them which are saved shall walk in the light of it: and the kings of the earth do bring their glory and honor into it. And the gates of it shall not be shut at all by day: for there shall be no night there. And they shall bring the glory and honor of the nations into it." (REV 21:24-26) There will be surviving nations who did not fall for the deceit of Satan after he was loosed from his thousand-year imprisonment! These nations will be those we will "rule and reign for ever and ever".

But many do follow Satan. A massive destruction occurs of millions who follow Satan's deception. When he is loosed, he convinces a great army of people from the nations to come against Christ. At this point, Jesus would have ruled on earth for one thousand years from Jerusalem – a place Ezekiel calls THE LORD IS THERE (EZ 48: 35). God wastes no time in handling this rebellion. There's a great whoosh of fire from heaven that devours them! Satan, Death and Hell are then cast into the lake of fire. And God conducts what is called the "great white throne" judgment of all unbelievers from the beginning of time (REV 20:12-15). Two different sets of books are opened at this judgment – the books recording the works of men and women as well as the Book of Life that has the names of those who are born-again believers.

Why would God use the Book of Life – with the names of believers in it - if this judgment is for unbelievers? Many, it seems, will claim to be Christ's followers, who never ran for their life God's way! "And why call ye me, Lord, Lord, and do not the things which I say?" (LK 6:46) "Not everyone that saith unto me Lord, Lord, shall enter into the kingdom of heaven; but he that doeth the will of my Father which is in heaven. Many will say to me in that day, "Lord, Lord have we not prophesied in thy name? And in thy name have cast out devils? And in thy name done many wonderful works?" And then I will profess unto them, I never knew you: depart from me ye that work iniquity." (MT 7:21-23). These masses are cast into the lake of fire, which is the eternal death.

Life will then proceed as God originally intended for His creation to live. The city will be about 1500 miles high, long, and wide. That's about 15 "atmosphere's" as we know them today (i.e. after 100 miles we're in outer space). The city will have a river flowing through its center, from top to bottom. It will come from the "throne of God and of the Lamb." And on either side of the river there will be the tree of life, which will bear twelve different fruits – a different one every month. The leaves of this tree "were for the healing of the nations." (REV 22:1-2) The leaves of the tree of life will "heal" the survivors of the disaster caused by the rebellion against Christ. God acted with great love when He sent Adam and Eve out of the garden so they could not eat of the tree of life – because they would have lived forever in sin – and us too! (GEN 3:22) God killed an animal to provide clothing to cover the nakedness of Adam and Eve. He would provide the blood of the Lamb to cover our sins. In REV 22:13, Jesus says, "I am the Alpha and Omega, the beginning and the end, the first and the last."

In the New Jerusalem, the tree of life is eaten freely. People live as God intended from the beginning with no more curse from sin (REV 22:3). God's home is with men and He shall wipe away all tears from their eyes. There shall be no more death, nor sorrow, nor crying, nor shall there be any more pain. The former things will all pass away and God will make everything new. (REV 21: 4-5)

"I come quickly; and my reward is with me to give to every man according as his work shall be." (REV 22:12,20) "The Spirit and the bride say Come. And let him that heareth say, Come. And let him that is athirst come. And whosoever will, let him take the water of life freely." (REV 22:17).

As we run for our lives God's way, let's remember the last recorded words of Christ in REV 22:20. They represent our divine Coach's last instructions, last invitation, last warning, and last promise: "Surely I come quickly." And John, speaking for all who are pressing toward the mark, for the Prize of the high calling of God, adds the last prayer: "Amen. Even so come, Lord Jesus."

"...the throne of God and of the Lamb shall be in it; and his servants shall serve him: And they shall see his face; and his name shall be in their foreheads. And there shall be no night there; and they need no candle, neither the light of the sun; for the Lord God giveth them light: and they shall reign forever and ever."

REV 22:3-5

INDEX

Other Books by Jim Biscardi Jr.

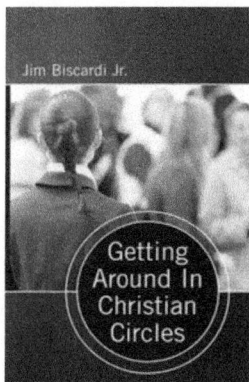

Jim Biscardi Jr.

Getting Around In Christian Circles

AMBUSHED
WILL THE REAL ENEMY PLEASE STAND UP?

Jim Biscardi, Jr.

THE MANTLE
How To Dress For Success In Leadership

Jim Biscardi, Jr.

What's in your future?
The Book of Revelation In Chronological Order

Jim Biscardi Jr.
Joe Velez

THE MANTLE
Leadership Teacher's Guide and Student Workbook

A STUDY OF CHRISTLIKE LEADERSHIP FOR HOME, CHURCH, WORKPLACE, SCHOOL, AND MAKING DISCIPLES

To be used with The Mantle: How To Dress For Success In Leadership

Jim Biscardi, Jr.

JIM BISCARDI JR.
FIRE in the SOUL
A Collection of Devotional Messages and Sermon-Starters